OUTLAWS, MOBSTERS & CROOKS

OUTLAWS, MOBSTERS & CROOKS

From the Old West to the Internet

VOLUME 1

Mobsters

•

Racketeers
& Gamblers

•

Robbers

Marie J. MacNee
Edited by Jane Hoehner

U·X·L ®

AN IMPRINT OF GALE

DETROIT · NEW YORK · LONDON

This book is dedicated, with love, to my parents

OUTLAWS, MOBSTERS & CROOKS: FROM THE OLD WEST TO THE INTERNET

by Marie J. MacNee

STAFF

Jane Hoehner, *U·X·L Senior Editor*
Carol DeKane Nagel, *U·X·L Managing Editor*
Thomas L. Romig, *U·X·L Publisher*

Shanna Heilveil, *Production Associate*
Evi Seoud, *Assistant Production Manager*
Mary Beth Trimper, *Production Director*

Jessica L. Ulrich, *Permissions Associate*
Margaret Chamberlain, *Permissions Specialist*

Michelle DiMercurio, *Art Director*
Tracey Rowens, *Senior Art Director*
Cynthia Baldwin, *Product Design Manager*
Barbara J. Yarrow, *Graphic Services Supervisor*

Marco Di Vita, Graphix Group, *Typesetting*

LIBRARY OF CONGRESS CATALOGING-IN-PUBLICATION DATA

MacNee, Marie J.
  Outlaws, mobsters & crooks: from the Old West to the Internet /
Marie J. MacNee : edited by Jane Hoehner.
    p. cm.
  Includes bibliographical references (p.   ) and index.
  Contents: v. 1. Mobsters, racketeers and gamblers, robbers — v.
2. Computer criminals, spies, swindlers, terrorists — v. 3. Bandits
and gunslingers, bootleggers, pirates.
  Summary: Presents the lives of seventy-five North American
criminals including the nature of their crimes, their motivations,
and information relating to the law officers who challenged them.
    ISBN 0-7876-2803-4 (set : acid-free paper). — ISBN 0-7876-2804-2
(vol. 1 : acid-free paper). — ISBN 0-7876-2805-0 (vol. 2 : acid
free paper). —ISBN 0-7876-2806-9 (vol. 3 : acid-free paper)
    1. Criminals—North America—Biography—Juvenile literature.
[1. Criminals.] I. Hoehner, Jane.   II. Title.   III. Title:
Outlaws, mobsters, and crooks.
HV6245.M232   1998
354.1'097—DC21

98-14861
CIP
AC

Contents

Volume 1

Battaglia rose from street crime to the top ranks of an underworld organization known as the Chicago Outfit before he received a prison sentence that ended his criminal career.

Operating in the early twentieth century, Black Hand gangsters were extortionists who preyed on Italian immigrants.

One of the nation's most powerful criminals, Capone seemed to be immune to the law until the government prosecuted him for tax evasion.

Born in Palermo, Sicily, Gambino was once head of the most powerful Mafia family in the United States.

Once a member of the notorious 42 Gang, Giancana worked his way to the top of the mob's Chicago Outfit, and was believed to have been responsible for hundreds of mob-related murders.

A powerful New York Mafia leader, "the Teflon don" seemed immune to the government's attempts to convict him until a close friend betrayed him.

Volume 2

Reader's Guide

"History is nothing more than a tableau of crimes and misfortunes," wrote eighteenth-century French writer Voltaire. There certainly is more to history than criminal deeds, misdemeanors, and misfortunes, but these offenses do offer fascinating lessons in history. The life stories of outlaws provide a glimpse into other times and other places, as well as provocative insight into contemporary issues.

Who's Included

Outlaws, Mobsters & Crooks: From the Old West to the Internet presents the life stories of seventy-three outlaws who lived (or committed crimes) in North America from the seventeenth century to the present day—from Blackbeard, the British-born pirate who terrorized the Carolina coast, to terrorist Timothy McVeigh.

Everyone's familiar with Bonnie and Clyde, Butch Cassidy, and Al Capone. But how many know the *whole* story: what their childhoods were like, what their first crime was, who worked with them—and against them—and how they ended up? *Outlaws, Mobsters & Crooks* offers a thorough and provocative look at the people and events involved in these stories.

Familiar figures such as Jesse James and Billy the Kid are present, as are lesser-known outlaws whose careers reveal much about the times in which they lived. Cattle Kate, for instance, was little more than a cattle rustler, but her story provides insight into the cattle wars of nineteenth-century Nebraska and the tensions that led to the Lincoln County War. Also included are outlaws such as Calamity Jane, whose main crime was unconventionality, and lawmen who sometimes stood on the wrong side of the law. The many men and women who have been labeled outlaws over the course of three centuries cannot all be profiled in one three-volume work. But those whose stories are told in *Outlaws, Mobsters & Crooks* include some of the best known, least known, weirdest, scariest, most despised, and least understood outlaws. In short, this work is intended as an overview of North American criminals—a jumping-off point for further inquiry.

LEGENDS, MYTHS, AND OUTRIGHT LIES

Many of the men and women profiled have been surrounded by legends that have grown to enormous proportions, making it very difficult to separate fact from fiction: Billy the Kid killed one man for every year of his life (he probably killed no more than six men); Jesse James lived to old age as a gentleman farmer (he was shot in the back of the head by Robert Ford at the age of thirty-four); Black Hand extortionists could bring bad luck to their victims simply by giving them "the evil eye" (they brought them bad luck, all right, but it was usually accomplished with a gun). In some cases, legends have fed on the published accounts of the criminals themselves—or the lawmen who pursued them. Some are accurate first-person accounts. Others are sensational exaggerations of true events—or wholesale fabrications. *Outlaws, Mobsters & Crooks* attempts to present a fair and complete picture of what is known about the lives and activities of the seventy-three outlaws profiled. When appropriate, entries mention the myths, unconventional theories, and alternate versions of accepted history that surround a particular outlaw—without suggesting they are truthful or fact-based.

ARRANGEMENT AND PRESENTATION

Outlaws, Mobsters & Crooks is arranged into three volumes. To enhance the usefulness of these volumes, the seventy-three entries have been grouped into ten categories: Mobsters, Racketeers and Gamblers, and Robbers (Volume 1); Computer Criminals, Spies, Swindlers, and Terrorists (Volume 2); and Bandits and Gunslingers, Bootleggers, and Pirates (Volume 3). Within each category, entries—which range from three to eleven pages in length—are arranged alphabetically by the outlaw's last name. The only exceptions to this arrangement are those outlaws who are listed by their "common" name, such as Billy the Kid or Black Bart; these entries are listed alphabetically by the first letter in that name. Aliases and birth names are presented when available. Each entry includes the birth and death dates of the subject (or the period during which he, she, or the gang was active).

Entries are lively, easy to read, and written in a straightforward style that is geared to challenge—but not frustrate—students. Difficult words are defined within the text; some words also include pronunciations. Technical words and legal terms are also explained within entries, enabling students to learn the vocabulary appropriate to a particular subject without having to consult other sources for definitions.

WHAT'S INSIDE

A detailed look at what they did, why they did it, and how their stories ended. Entries focus on the entire picture—not just the headline news—to provide the following sorts of information:

- **Personal background:** interesting details about the subject's family, upbringing, and youth

- **Crimes and misdeeds:** an in-depth look at the subject's outlaw history

- **Aftermath:** from jail time, to legal and illegal executions, to mysterious disappearances, entries relate what happened after the dirty deeds were done

- **A look at the other side of the law:** Many entries also provide extensive information on the other side of the law, for example, the brilliant astronomer who tracked a West German hacker, the FBI agents who hounded John Dillinger and Al Capone, and the frontier judge who earned the nickname "the hanging judge."

ADDED FEATURES

Outlaws, Mobsters & Crooks includes a number of additional features that help make the connection between people, places, and historic events.

- A timeline at the beginning of each volume provides a listing of outlaw landmarks and important international events.

- Sidebars provide fascinating supplemental information, such as sketches of criminal associates, profiles of law enforcement officials and agencies, and explanations of the political and social scenes of the era, for example, the anti-communist hysteria that consumed the United States at the time of the Rosenberg trial. Sidebars also offer a contemporary perspective of people and events through excerpts of letters written by the outlaw profiled, citations from newspapers and journals of the day, and much more.

- Quotes—both by and about the outlaw—offer revealing insights into their lives and times.

- 117 photographs and illustrations bring the outlaws to life.

- Suggestions for related books and movies—both fictional and fact-based—are liberally sprinkled throughout the entries.

- A list of sources for further reading at the end of each entry lists books, newspaper and magazine articles, and Internet addresses for additional and bibliographical information.

- A comprehensive index at the end of each volume provides easy access to the people, places, and events mentioned throughout *Outlaws, Mobsters & Crooks: From the Old West to the Internet.*

SPECIAL THANKS

The author would like to thank U•X•L Senior Editor Jane Hoehner, Permissions Associate Jessica L. Ulrich, and the research staff—particularly Maureen Richards—of Gale Research for their invaluable help and guidance. The author would also like to thank the staff of the Grosse Pointe Library for their gracious assistance.

COMMENTS AND SUGGESTIONS

We welcome your comments on this work as well as suggestions for personalities to be featured in future editions of *Outlaws, Mobsters & Crooks: From the Old West to the Internet.* Please write: Editors, *Outlaws, Mobsters & Crooks,* U•X•L, 835 Penobscot Building, Detroit, Michigan, 48226-4094; call toll-free: 1 (800) 877-4253; or fax (313) 877-6348.

Outlaws Alphabetically

Italic number indicates volume number

Timeline

Spring 1718: Edward Teach—also known as **Blackbeard**—and his crew of pirates blockade the city of Charleston, South Carolina.

November 1718: Thomas Spotswood, the governor of Virginia, issues a proclamation offering rewards for the capture—dead or alive—of **Blackbeard** and his shipmates.

November 22, 1718: A navy crew led by Lieutenant Robert Maynard attacks **Blackbeard**'s pirate ship near the Carolina coast. The severed head of Blackbeard is hung from the bowsprit of the navy ship.

1720: Captain Woodes Rogers, the governor of the Bahamas, issues a proclamation naming Calico Jack Rackam, **Anne Bonny,** and Mary Read as enemies of England.

May 9, 1800: Joseph Baker and two other pirates are hanged in a public execution in Philadelphia, Pennsylvania.

March 11, 1831: Charles Gibbs and Thomas G. Wansley are convicted of murder and piracy in New York.

March 19, 1831: An Englishman named Edward Smith commits the first bank heist in American history when he robs the City Bank in New York City.

April 22, 1831: Pirates **Charles Gibbs** and Thomas G. Wansley are hanged on Ellis Island in New York in front of thousands of onlookers.

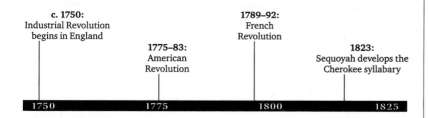

c. 1750:
Industrial Revolution
begins in England

1775–83:
American
Revolution

1789–92:
French
Revolution

1823:
Sequoyah develops the
Cherokee syllabary

| 1750 | 1775 | 1800 | 1825 |

July 11, 1859: Gold thief **Richard Barter** is shot and killed by Sheriff J. Boggs in the California foothills.

1861: Shortly after the Civil War breaks out, **Elizabeth Van Lew,** a Union sympathizer who lives inside the Confederacy, begins to send information about the Southern war effort to Northern officers.

February 13, 1866: Jesse James and the James-Younger Gang rob the Clay County Savings and Loan Bank in Liberty, Missouri.

April 5, 1866: Bill Miner enters San Quentin penitentiary after being convicted of armed robbery. He is released after serving a little more than four years of his sentence.

January 23, 1871: Bill Miner and two accomplices rob a California stagecoach using stolen guns. He returns to San Quentin the following June.

October 9, 1871: Swindler **Sophie Lyons** is convicted of grand larceny and sentenced to serve time in Sing Sing prison.

December 19, 1872: Sophie Lyons escapes from Sing Sing prison using a forged key.

1873: The James-Younger Gang commits its first train robbery.

1874: Gunslinger **Clay Allison** commits his first recorded killing.

July 26, 1875: Charles Boles—better known as **Black Bart**—commits the first in a series of stagecoach robberies near Copperopolis, California.

August 3, 1877: Black Bart robs his fourth stagecoach, leaving behind a poem signed "Black Bart, the PO 8 [poet]."

1878: Martha Jane Cannary—known as **Calamity Jane**—acts as a nurse during a smallpox epidemic in Deadwood, Dakota Territory.

1861–65: American Civil War

1868: The Fourteenth Amendment to the Constitution of the United States is adopted

| 1850 | 1855 | 1860 | 1865 |

Spring 1878: Sam Bass and his gang stage four train holdups around Dallas, Texas.

April 1, 1878: William Bonney—also known as **Billy the Kid**—participates in an ambush that kills Sheriff William Brady in Lincoln County, New Mexico.

July 15, 1878: Texas Rangers wound and capture robber **Sam Bass** in Round Rock, Texas.

1879: Bartholomew "Bat" Masterson is appointed deputy U.S. marshal.

October 7, 1879: The second James Gang robs a train near Glendale, Missouri, of $35,000.

December 1879: Wyatt Earp arrives in lawless Tombstone, Arizona, and is soon joined by brothers James, Morgan, Virgil, and Warren.

July 14, 1880: Bill Miner is released from San Quentin prison after serving nine years for stagecoach robbery. He returns to the California prison the following year.

April 11, 1881: Dallas Stoudenmire becomes marshal of El Paso, Texas.

May 13, 1881: Convicted of murder, **Billy the Kid** is sentenced to hang.

May 25, 1881: Livestock rustler **Curly Bill,** otherwise known as William Brocius, is shot in the mouth during an argument with lawman William Breakenridge.

July 14, 1881: Sheriff Pat Garrett shoots and kills **Billy the Kid.**

October 26, 1881: Wyatt Earp and brothers Morgan and Virgil, joined by Doc Holliday, confront the Clantons and McLauries at the O.K. Corral. The gunfight leaves three men dead.

1877:
Thomas Edison is awarded the patent for the phonograph

1880:
The Metropolitan Museum of Art opens in New York City

1870   1873   1876   1879

April 3, 1882: Jesse James dies in St. Joseph, Missouri, after fellow outlaw Robert Ford shoots him in the back of the head.

June 1882: Pressured by city officials, **Dallas Stoudenmire** resigns from his post as marshal of El Paso.

September 18, 1882: Dallas Stoudenmire is shot and killed during a saloon brawl.

1883: Belle Starr is the first woman ever to be tried for a major crime in Judge Isaac Parker's infamous "court of the damned."

November 1883: Black Bart is captured in San Francisco, California. He pleads guilty to robbery and is sentenced to six years at San Quentin penitentiary.

October 6, 1885: Swindler **Ellen Peck** is convicted of forging a document to obtain $3,000 from the Mutual Life Insurance Company of New York. She is sentenced to four-and-a-half years in prison.

July 3, 1887: Clay Allison dies when he is run over by a freight wagon.

November 3, 1887: Robert Leroy Parker—better known as **Butch Cassidy**—and members of the McCarty Gang botch a robbery of the Denver and Rio Grande Express train in Colorado.

1889: Maverick calves stolen from the herds of Wyoming cattle barons find their way into the corral of **Cattle Kate**.

February 3, 1889: Belle Starr is ambushed and killed near her home in the Indian Territory by an unidentified gunman.

March 30, 1889: Butch Cassidy and other gang members rob the First National Bank of Denver of $20,000 in bank notes.

July 20, 1889: Cattle baron Albert J. Bothwell organizes a group to put an end to **Cattle Kate** and James Averill's cattle rustling. Watson and Averill are lynched.

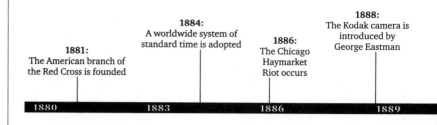

1881:
The American branch of the Red Cross is founded

1884:
A worldwide system of standard time is adopted

1886:
The Chicago Haymarket Riot occurs

1888:
The Kodak camera is introduced by George Eastman

1880   1883   1886   1889

1890s: Black Hand Society extortionists prey on Italian immigrants by threatening violence if their victims do not pay. The Black Hand reign of terror continues for approximately thirty years in Italian Harlem.

1890s: Swindler **Sophie Lyons** opens the New York Women's Banking and Investment Company with fellow con artist Carrie Morse. Before closing, the operation collects at least $50,000 from unsuspecting victims.

November 4, 1890: Marion Hedgepeth and other gangsters rob the Missouri Pacific train near Omaha, Nebraska. The following week they strike the Chicago, Milwaukee & St. Paul train just outside of Milwaukee, Wisconsin.

1892: After a long delay, **Marion Hedgepeth** is tried and convicted of train robbery. He is sentenced to serve twelve to twenty-five years in the state penitentiary.

1894: Posing as the wife of a Danish navy officer, **Ellen Peck** collects more than $50,000 from various banks.

July 4, 1894: Butch Cassidy is tried for cattle rustling. He is convicted and imprisoned.

July 28, 1895: Five young men, known as the **Buck Gang,** begin a murderous thirteen-day crime spree in the Indian Territory to the west of Arkansas.

August 10, 1895: All five members of the **Buck Gang** are captured and taken into custody.

1896: Calamity Jane works for an amusement company in Minneapolis, Minnesota, dressed as an army scout.

January 19, 1896: Butch Cassidy is released from the Wyoming State Penitentiary.

July 1, 1896: Rufus Buck and four other **Buck Gang** members are executed in a mass hanging at Fort Smith, Arkansas.

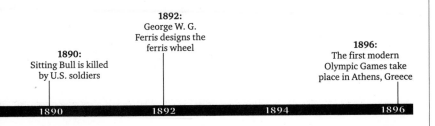

1890:
Sitting Bull is killed by U.S. soldiers

1892:
George W. G. Ferris designs the ferris wheel

1896:
The first modern Olympic Games take place in Athens, Greece

1890   1892   1894   1896

1897: Cassie Chadwick is released from prison after serving three years for fraud. She soon begins to swindle banks by claiming to be the illegitimate daughter of millionaire Andrew Carnegie.

1899: Pearl Hart and Joe Boot rob the Globe stage in the Arizona Territory—in what is recognized as the last American stagecoach robbery.

1900: When Mads Albert Sorenson dies in Chicago, his wife, **Belle Gunness,** is suspected of foul play.

May 1900: Found living in a brothel, **Calamity Jane** travels to Buffalo, New York, where she takes a job performing in a Western show at the Pan-American Exposition.

September 25, 1900: Union spy **Elizabeth Van Lew** dies in Richmond, Virginia, at the age of seventy-two.

July 3, 1901: Butch Cassidy and the Wild Bunch raid the Great Northern Flyer train near Wagner, Montana. It is the gang's final heist.

December 19, 1902: Pearl Hart leaves Yuma prison following an eighteen-month imprisonment.

August 1, 1903: Ravaged by alcoholism, **Calamity Jane** dies near Deadwood, Dakota Territory.

September 13, 1904: Bill Miner and others rob an express train outside of Vancouver, Canada.

December 7, 1904: Swindler **Cassie Chadwick** is arrested in New York. She is later convicted of six counts of fraud and sentenced to ten years in the Ohio State Penitentiary.

1905: Wealthy Brooklyn, New York, butcher Gaetano Costa refuses to pay a **Black Hand** extortionist and is shot to death in his shop.

1898:
The Spanish-American War begins

1902:
Cuba achieves independence

1903:
The Hay-Bunau-Varilla Treaty is negotiated, giving the U.S. control of the Panama Canal

1898   1900   1902   1904

1906: Cassie Chadwick dies at the age of forty-eight in the prison hospital at Ohio State Penitentiary.

1906: Belle Gunness begins to place personal ads in newspapers in Chicago and other cities in the Midwest to lure wealthy men to her Indiana farm.

1908: Joseph Weil works with Fred "the Deacon" Buckminster to trick clients into paying to have them paint buildings with a phony waterproofing substance. It is the first in a series of scams committed by Weil over the next twenty-five years.

April 28, 1908: After the farmhouse belonging to **Belle Gunness** burns to the ground, authorities discover the decapitated corpse of a woman in the ruins.

May 22, 1908: Ray Lamphere, **Belle Gunness**'s farmhand, is tried and acquitted of murder. Convicted of arson, he is sentenced to up to twenty years in prison.

1910: The six **Genna brothers**—later known as "the Terrible Gennas"—arrive in the United States from Marsala, Sicily.

January 1, 1910: Former train robber **Marion Hedgepeth** is killed by a policeman during an attempted saloon robbery.

February 22, 1911: Bill Miner commits his last train robbery at Sulfur Springs, Georgia, at the age of sixty-four.

1912: Mexican General Victoriano Huerta condemns soldier **Pancho Villa** to death. A stay of execution is later issued.

1912: The **Genna brothers** become involved in **Black Hand Society** activities in Chicago.

November 6, 1912: Eleven members of New York's Hudson Dusters Gang ambush rival gangster **Owney Madden** at a Manhattan dance hall. Left for dead, Madden lives.

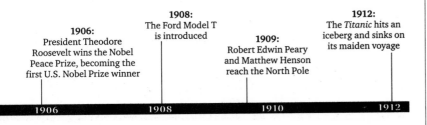

1906:
President Theodore Roosevelt wins the Nobel Peace Prize, becoming the first U.S. Nobel Prize winner

1908:
The Ford Model T is introduced

1909:
Robert Edwin Peary and Matthew Henson reach the North Pole

1912:
The *Titanic* hits an iceberg and sinks on its maiden voyage

1906   1908   1910   1912

1913: Forty-one-year-old **Diamond Joe Esposito** spends $65,000 to celebrate his marriage to sixteen-year old Carmela Marchese.

1913: *Why Crime Does Not Pay,* the autobiography of veteran swindler **Sophie Lyons,** is published.

September 2, 1913: Veteran stagecoach and train robber **Bill Miner** dies in a prison hospital in Georgia.

November 28, 1914: Owney Madden kills rival New York gangster Patsy Doyle. Sentenced to twenty years for the murder, he is released after serving nine years.

March 9, 1916: Pancho Villa and a gang of Villistas (followers of Villa) attack a small New Mexico border town and military camp, killing seventeen Americans.

1917: The obituary of stagecoach robber **Black Bart** appears in New York newspapers. Some people suspect that the death notice is a hoax engineered by the outlaw.

May 24, 1918: Bugs Moran is convicted of armed robbery and sentenced to serve time at Joliet State Prison in Illinois.

November 24, 1918: Bank robbers **Margie Dean** and husband Dale Jones are shot to death in their car by police near Los Angeles, California.

1919: Racketeer **Arnold Rothstein** masterminds the "Black Sox scandal"—the fixing of the 1919 World Series.

1919: Al Capone, a gunman for New York's notorious James Street Gang, moves to Chicago to escape arrest on a murder charge.

December 1919: Swindler **Charles Ponzi** launches an eight-month get-rich-quick scam using international postal reply coupons.

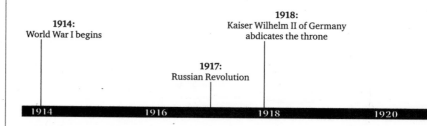

1914:
World War I begins

1917:
Russian Revolution

1918:
Kaiser Wilhelm II of Germany abdicates the throne

| 1914 | 1916 | 1918 | 1920 |

1920: A grand jury meets in Chicago to investigate the 1919 Black Sox scandal.

1920: The **Genna brothers** turn Chicago's Little Italy into a vast moonshine operation.

May 8, 1924: Former swindler **Sophie Lyons** is attacked in her home. She dies later that evening in Grace Hospital in Detroit.

September 6, 1924: **John Dillinger** and Edgar Singleton rob an Indiana grocer, for which Dillinger is later sentenced to ten to twenty years in prison.

November 10, 1924: Chicago gangster Charles Dion O'Banion is assassinated in his North Side flower shop.

1925: **Charles Ponzi** is released from prison after serving four years in a Plymouth, Massachusetts, prison for mail fraud.

January 12, 1925: O'Banion gangsters attempt to ambush **Al Capone** by firing into the gangster's limousine. Capone is not injured.

January 24, 1925: Johnny Torrio, who rules Chicago's South Side bootlegging empire with **Al Capone,** is ambushed by rival gangsters.

June 13, 1925: A car filled with Genna gunmen ambushes **Bugs Moran** and Vincent "the Schemer" Drucci on Michigan Avenue in downtown Chicago. Both are wounded—but not killed.

September 20, 1926: Chicago gangster **Hymie Weiss** leads a squad of North Side gangsters in an attempt to ambush **Al Capone** at the Hawthorne Inn, the gangster's Cicero head-quarters. Although more than one thousand bullets rip into the building, Capone escapes without injury.

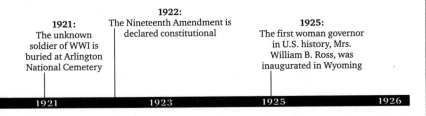

1921:
The unknown soldier of WWI is buried at Arlington National Cemetery

1922:
The Nineteenth Amendment is declared constitutional

1925:
The first woman governor in U.S. history, Mrs. William B. Ross, was inaugurated in Wyoming

1921　　　　　1923　　　　　1925　　　　　1926

1927: Wanted in connection with a robbery, **Ma Barker**'s boy, Herman, commits suicide during a battle with police in Wichita, Kansas.

1928: The **Purple Gang** trial ends the Cleaners and Dyers War in Detroit.

March 21, 1928: Joe Esposito dies near his Chicago home when machine-gunners fire on him from a car. Esposito is struck by fifty-eight bullets.

November 4, 1928: Racketeer **Arnold Rothstein** is shot at the Park Central Hotel in New York. He dies two days later.

1929: Twenty-year old **Irene Schroeder** abandons her husband to run away with Walter Glenn Dague. The couple soon rob a number of stores and small banks.

January 13, 1929: Former lawman **Wyatt Earp** dies in California at the age of eighty, having outlived his four brothers.

February 14, 1929: Members of **Al Capone**'s gang masquerade as policemen raiding a garage on North Clark Street in Chicago. The St. Valentine's Day Massacre leaves seven people dead.

June 13, 1929: Legs Diamond and his enforcer, Charles Entratta, kill two men at the Hotsy Totsy Club, a Manhattan speakeasy.

1930s: Meyer Lansky, Lucky Luciano, and others work together to help solidify a nationwide crime syndicate. Many former bootleggers and members of gangs such as Detroit's **Purple Gang** join the national syndicate.

November 17, 1930: Sam Battaglia robs Mrs. William Hale Thompson—the wife of the governor of Illinois—of more than $15,000 in jewels.

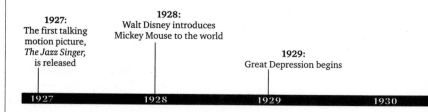

1927:
The first talking motion picture, *The Jazz Singer*, is released

1928:
Walt Disney introduces Mickey Mouse to the world

1929:
Great Depression begins

1927   1928   1929   1930

1931: Veteran gangster Joe "the Boss" Maseria is assassinated in a restaurant in Coney Island, New York. **Bugsy Siegel** is among the hitmen.

February 23, 1931: Irene Schroeder is executed at Rockview penitentiary in Pennsylvania. Her partner, Walter Glenn Dague, is executed a few days later.

April 1931: Legs Diamond is shot several times in a drive-by ambush. He survives.

June 1931: Federal officials charge Chicago gangster **Al Capone** with income tax evasion.

September 16, 1931: Three unarmed men are shot to death by **Purple Gang** mobsters. The incident is known as the Collingwood Manor Massacre.

October 1931: Al Capone is convicted of income tax evasion and sentenced to eleven years in prison.

December 17, 1931: Legs Diamond is shot dead by rival gangsters in his hotel room in Albany, New York.

1932: Gangster **Owney Madden** is released from Sing Sing prison. Later that year he is jailed again for parole violation. Released, he retires from the New York underworld.

February 2, 1932: Clyde Barrow is paroled from Eastham prison farm in Ohio—vowing that he will die before returning to prison. Barrow rejoins **Bonnie Parker** and the two embark on a two-year crime spree.

February 8, 1932: Dutch Schultz's gunmen murder Vincent Coll as Coll makes a call from a phone booth.

1931:
The *Star-Spangled Banner* becomes the national anthem of the United States

1932:
Amelia Earhart becomes the first woman to cross the Atlantic in a solo flight

1931   1932

1933: FBI agent Melvin Purvis arrests Chicago gangster **Roger Touhy** for the kidnapping of millionaire William A. Hamm, Jr. Touhy is cleared of the kidnapping, which was engineered by members of the Barker-Karpis Gang.

1933: Murder, Inc.—an enforcement division of the national crime syndicate—is formed under the leadership of **Louis Lepke.**

May 22, 1933: Thanks in part to a petition by friends and relatives, **John Dillinger** is released early from the Michigan City prison in Indiana.

July 22, 1933: Machine Gun Kelly and Albert Bates kidnap oil millionaire Charles F. Urschel from his Oklahoma City mansion.

September 26, 1933: Memphis, Tennessee, police detectives capture kidnappers **Machine Gun Kelly** and Albert Bates.

September 26, 1933: Using guns smuggled by **John Dillinger,** ten prisoners escape from the Michigan City penitentiary in Indiana. Bank robber Harry Pierpont is among the escaped convicts.

1934: Swindler **Charles Ponzi** is deported to Italy as an undesirable alien.

January 1934: The Dillinger Gang falls apart when police arrest **John Dillinger** and others in Tucson, Arizona. Dillinger is extradited to Indiana.

May 23, 1934: Bonnie and Clyde are killed by lawmen as they drive down a back road near Arcadia, Louisiana.

July 22, 1934: Tipped off by the "Lady in Red," FBI agents apprehend **John Dillinger** as he leaves Chicago's Biograph Theater. The gangster, who is recognized as Public Enemy Number One, is shot dead.

1933:
The Twenty-first
Amendment ends
Prohibition

1934:
American child
star Shirley
Temple makes
her first movie

1933   1934

1935: Two Gun Alterie is called as a government witness in the income tax evasion trial of Ralph "Bottles" Capone (brother of **Al Capone**).

1935: New York mayor Fiorello LaGuardia and district attorney Thomas E. Dewey join forces to destroy **Dutch Schultz**'s slot machine empire. Schultz later vows to kill Dewey.

1935: Ray Hamilton, a former associate of outlaws **Bonnie and Clyde,** is put to death in the electric chair.

January 8, 1935: Arthur "Doc" Barker, wanted for killing a night watchman, is captured in Chicago by FBI agent Melvin Purvis.

January 16, 1935: After a four-hour gun battle, **Ma Barker** and her son Fred are killed by lawmen near Lake Weir, Florida.

July 18, 1935: Former bootlegger **Two Gun Alterie** is killed in a machine-gun ambush.

October 23, 1935: Dutch Schultz, a member of the board of the national crime syndicate, is ambushed in a Newark, New Jersey, chophouse with three associates.

1936: Juliet Stuart Poyntz, an American communist and Soviet spy, is seen in Moscow in the company of fellow American and convicted spy George Mink.

May 1936: Alvin Karpis, a member of the Barker-Karpis Gang, is captured in New Orleans, Louisiana. FBI director J. Edgar Hoover personally places him under arrest.

1939: Gangster **Frank Costello** is tried in New Orleans, Louisiana, on charges of tax evasion. The government loses its case because of lack of evidence.

August 24, 1939: Racketeer **Louis Lepke** surrenders to the FBI through newspaper columnist Walter Winchell.

1935:
The Social Security Act is signed by President Franklin D. Roosevelt

1936:
Spanish Civil War begins

1939:
World War II begins

1935   1936   1937   1938

1940: Joseph Weil is sentenced to three years in prison for a mail-fraud charge involving phony oil leases. It is the veteran swindler's final conviction.

October 9, 1942: Roger Touhy and six other prisoners escape from Joliet penitentiary. The escaped convicts are soon placed on the FBI's Most Wanted list.

December 1942: FBI agents capture **Roger Touhy** at a boardinghouse in Chicago.

1943: American Communist Party member **Julius Rosenberg** is recruited by KGB agent Aleksander Feklisov to spy for the Soviet Union.

March 4, 1944: Murder, Inc., chief **Louis Lepke** is executed in the electric chair at Sing Sing prison.

1945: Meyer Lansky and **Bugsy Siegel** begin to establish a gambling hotel in a small western town called Las Vegas, Nevada.

June 1945: Julius Rosenberg arranges for his brother-in-law, David Greenglass, to provide a courier with classified information about the A-bomb.

December 1946: At a gangster summit in Havana, Cuba, **Bugsy Siegel** swears to fellow syndicate members that he has not stolen mob money through his Las Vegas gambling operation.

January 25, 1947: Retired gangster **Al Capone** dies at his mansion in Palm Island, Florida.

June 20, 1947: Bugsy Siegel is shot to death in the living room of **Virginia Hill**'s Beverly Hills mansion.

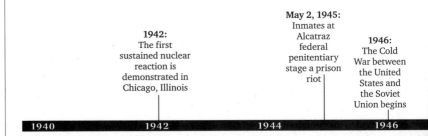

1942:
The first sustained nuclear reaction is demonstrated in Chicago, Illinois

May 2, 1945:
Inmates at Alcatraz federal penitentiary stage a prison riot

1946:
The Cold War between the United States and the Soviet Union begins

| 1940 | 1942 | 1944 | 1946 |

1949: Lloyd Barker, the only surviving member of the Barker Gang, is shot to death by his wife.

January 1949: Charles Ponzi dies in the charity ward of a Brazilian hospital at the age of sixty-six.

1950s: Working under **Sam Giancana, Sam Battaglia** becomes chief of the Chicago Outfit's narcotics operations.

May 10, 1950: The Senate Special Committee to Investigate Organized Crime in Interstate Commerce, spearheaded by Senator Estes Kefauver, subpoenas the testimony of numerous gangsters in a year-long attempt to piece together an accurate picture of organized crime in America.

June 15, 1950: Questioned by the FBI, David Greenglass implicates his sister, **Ethel Rosenberg,** and her husband, **Julius,** in espionage.

May 1951: "Queen of the Mob" **Virginia Hill** appears as a key witness before the Kefauver Committee and shocks committee members with her candid responses.

March 6, 1951: Ethel and Julius Rosenberg are tried for conspiracy to commit espionage.

June 19, 1953: In spite of worldwide pleas for clemency, **Ethel and Julius Rosenberg** are electrocuted at Sing Sing prison.

1954: Bank robber and kidnapper **Machine Gun Kelly** suffers a fatal heart attack in Leavenworth prison.

June 23, 1954: A federal grand jury charges **Virginia Hill** with income tax evasion.

1956: Retired swindler **Joseph Weil** is called to testify before a Senate subcommittee, led by Senator Estes Kefauver, investigating juvenile delinquency.

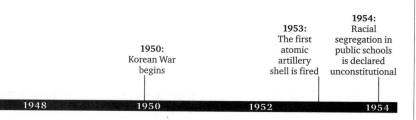

1950:
Korean War
begins

1953:
The first
atomic
artillery
shell is fired

1954:
Racial
segregation in
public schools
is declared
unconstitutional

1948   1950   1952   1954

1957: Bugs Moran dies from cancer in Leavenworth penitentiary, where he is serving time for bank robbery.

October 25, 1957: Mobster Albert Anastasia is shot to death in the barber shop of the Park Sheraton Hotel in New York City. Rival gangsters **Carlo Gambino** and Vito Genovese are believed to be responsible for ordering the murder.

1959: FBI agents plant a microphone in the backroom of the Forest Park, Illinois, headquarters of mobster **Sam Giancana.**

November 25, 1959: Convicted kidnapper **Roger Touhy** is released from prison after the kidnapping he was found guilty of is revealed to have been a hoax.

December 17, 1959: Former bootlegger **Roger Touhy** is gunned down near his sister's Chicago home.

1960s: The U.S. government begins to subpoena gangster **Carlo Gambino** to appear before the grand jury to investigate his decades-long involvement in organized crime.

1965: After refusing to testify about the mob's activities before a federal grand jury in Chicago, mobster **Sam Giancana** is sentenced to one year in prison.

March 25, 1966: Virginia Hill dies from an overdose of sleeping pills near Salzburg, Austria.

December 1969: Diana Oughton, a former social activist, attends a secret meeting of the Weathermen, a terrorist organization, in Flint, Michigan.

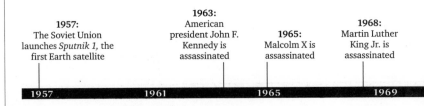

1957:
The Soviet Union launches *Sputnik 1,* the first Earth satellite

1963:
American president John F. Kennedy is assassinated

1965:
Malcolm X is assassinated

1968:
Martin Luther King Jr. is assassinated

1957   1961   1965   1969

1970: JoAnne Chesimard—also known as Assata Shakur—joins the Black Panther Party.

March 1970: Diana Oughton dies as a bomb explodes in a house in New York City. The house is a bomb factory for Weathermen terrorists.

March 23, 1971: Author **Clifford Irving** signs a contract with McGraw-Hill publishing company to write an authorized biography of billionaire Howard Hughes, who has not been interviewed by journalists since 1958.

November 1971: D. B. Cooper hijacks Northwest Airlines flight 305.

December 1971: Employees of **Jerry Schneider** inform officials at the Pacific Telephone & Telegraph company in Los Angeles, California, that their boss is using access to the phone company's computerized inventory system to order products illegally.

February 1972: Investigators for the Los Angeles District Attorney obtain a search warrant for the business of **Jerry Schneider.** Schneider is later charged with receiving stolen property and sentenced to two months in prison.

March 9, 1972: Author **Clifford Irving** is charged with federal conspiracy to defraud, forgery, and several other charges for writing the fake autobiography of Howard Hughes.

1973: Mobster **Sam Battaglia** dies in prison, having served six years of a fifteen-year sentence for extortion.

February 18, 1973: Retired mobster **Frank Costello** dies of natural causes at the age of eighty-two.

July 4, 1973: "To my people"—a speech in which **JoAnne Chesimard** describes herself as a black revolutionary—is publicly broadcast.

1972:
The Watergate affair—the burglary of Democratic headquarters in Washington, D.C., takes place

1973:
Skylab, the first U.S. space station, is launched

1970   1971   1972   1973

1974: JoAnne Chesimard and fellow Black Liberation Army member Fred Hilton are tried and acquitted of a 1972 bank robbery in New York.

February 4, 1974: Newspaper heiress **Patty Hearst** is kidnapped by members of the Symbionese Liberation Army (SLA).

April 5, 1974: Patty Hearst records a message to announce publicly that she has joined the SLA.

July 29, 1974: College dropout **Christopher Boyce** begins work at TRW Systems, an aerospace firm that works on many classified military programs. The following year Boyce and friend **Andrew Daulton Lee** devise a plan to provide Soviet agents with top-secret information.

June 2, 1975: John Gotti pleads guilty to attempted manslaughter in the second degree for the murder of James McBratney in Staten Island, New York.

September 18, 1975: Patty Hearst is captured with terrorist Wendy Yoshimura in an apartment in San Francisco.

October 15, 1975: Mobster **Carlo Gambino** dies of a heart attack at his home in Long Island, New York, at the age of seventy-three.

October 10, 1976: Convicted telephone thief **Jerry Schneider** appears on a *60 Minutes* television segment called "Dial E for Embezzlement."

1977: Gordon Kahl, a member of the conservative survivalist group called Posse Comitatus, is convicted of failing to file federal income tax returns. He is placed on probation.

March 25, 1977: JoAnne Chesimard is convicted of the murder of a New Jersey state trooper. She is sentenced to life in prison plus more than twenty-five years.

April 1977: Christopher Boyce and Andrew Daulton Lee— the Falcon and the Snowman—are tried for espionage. Both are convicted.

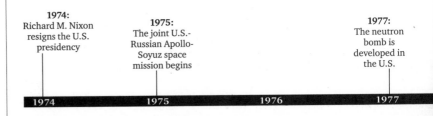

1974:
Richard M. Nixon resigns the U.S. presidency

1975:
The joint U.S.-Russian Apollo-Soyuz space mission begins

1977:
The neutron bomb is developed in the U.S.

| 1974 | 1975 | 1976 | 1977 |

November 5, 1978: FBI agents arrest computer thief **Stanley Rifkin** in Carlsbad, California.

January 1979: President Jimmy Carter commutes the prison sentence of convicted bank robber **Patty Hearst.**

February 13, 1979: Released on bail, computer thief **Stanley Rifkin** is arrested for initiating a wire fraud of the Union Bank of Los Angeles. A month later he is convicted of two counts of wire fraud and is sentenced to eight years in federal prison.

November 2, 1979: Convicted murderer **JoAnne Chesimard** escapes from the New Jersey Corrections Institute for women. She later flees to Cuba.

January 1980: Convicted spy **Christopher Boyce** escapes from a federal prison in Lompoc, California. Nineteen months later he is captured and returned to prison—with ninety years added to his original sentence.

April 1980: Two children discover a package containing several dozen $20 bills near Portland, Oregon. The serial numbers are traced to the ransom payment in the **D. B. Cooper** hijacking.

May 28, 1980: John Favara, the man responsible for the accidental killing of gangster **John Gotti**'s twelve-year-old son, disappears. He is never seen again.

January 15, 1983: **Meyer Lansky** dies of cancer in a New York hospital at the age of eighty-one.

February 13, 1983: Federal marshals attempt to serve tax evader **Gordon Kahl** with a warrant for violating parole. A shootout follows, in which two marshals are killed.

May 11, 1983: **Gordon Kahl** and two others are charged with the murders of two federal marshals.

June 4, 1983: **Gordon Kahl** dies in a shootout with federal marshals near Smithville, Arkansas.

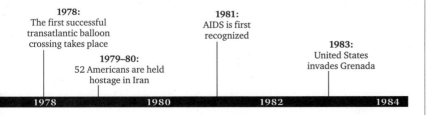

1978:
The first successful transatlantic balloon crossing takes place

1979–80:
52 Americans are held hostage in Iran

1981:
AIDS is first recognized

1983:
United States invades Grenada

1978   1980   1982   1984

April 1985: CIA agent **Aldrich Ames** begins to work as a Soviet spy.

June 2, 1986: San Francisco peace activist **Katya Komisaruk** destroys a government computer on the Vandenberg Air Force base as an anti-nuclear protest.

August 1986: Astronomer Clifford Stoll discovers a seventy-five cent shortfall in his computer system's accounting records. He later discovers that the shortfall is due to an unauthorized user who has broken into the system to access classified information without being traced.

March 13, 1987: Gangster **John Gotti** is tried on charges of racketeering. The "Teflon don" is acquitted.

November 1987: Katya Komisaruk is tried on one count of destruction of government property. During her trial, many supporters appear in court carrying white roses as a symbol of solidarity.

January 11, 1988: Convicted of destroying government property, **Katya Komisaruk** is sentenced to five years in federal prison.

March 2, 1989: Clifford Stoll's investigation of computer records leads to a spy ring of West German computer hackers. **Marcus Hess** and two others are arrested in Hanover, West Germany.

July 1989: Computer hacker **Kevin Mitnick** is sentenced to one year in federal prison at Lompoc, California, for breaking into telephone company computers and stealing long-distance access codes.

1992: John Gotti is tried and convicted of fourteen counts of racketeering and murder after being betrayed by former aide Salvatore "Sammy the Bull" Gravano.

May 12, 1993: The FBI begins a criminal investigation of **Aldrich Ames,** who is suspected of spying for the Soviets.

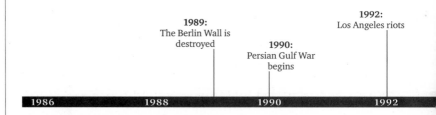

1989:
The Berlin Wall is destroyed

1990:
Persian Gulf War begins

1992:
Los Angeles riots

1986   1988   1990   1992

February 21, 1994: Soviet spy **Aldrich Ames** is arrested as he drives to work at CIA headquarters. He is later convicted of espionage and sentenced to life in prison.

December 24, 1994: Convicted hacker **Kevin Mitnick** steals data from the home computer of computer security expert Tsutomu Shimomura.

February 15, 1995: Federal agents arrest **Kevin Mitnick** in Raleigh, North Carolina, without a struggle.

April 19, 1995: A bomb explodes in front of the Alfred P. Murrah Federal Building in Oklahoma City, Oklahoma, killing 168 people. **Timothy McVeigh** is arrested a short time later.

November 21, 1996: Archaeologists find what they believe to be the long-lost flagship of **Blackbeard** the pirate.

April 1997: The trial of suspected terrorist **Timothy McVeigh** begins in Denver, Colorado.

June 2, 1997: **Timothy McVeigh** is convicted of all eleven charges against him involving the Oklahoma City bombing.

December 1997: A group of hackers break into an Internet site and leave behind a computerized ransom note threatening to release a computer virus if **Kevin Mitnick** is not set free.

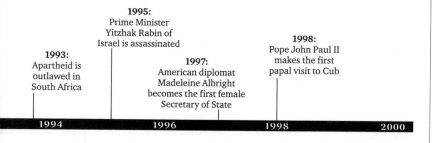

1993:
Apartheid is outlawed in South Africa

1995:
Prime Minister Yitzhak Rabin of Israel is assassinated

1997:
American diplomat Madeleine Albright becomes the first female Secretary of State

1998:
Pope John Paul II makes the first papal visit to Cub

1994   1996   1998   2000

Picture Credits

The photographs and illustrations appearing in *Outlaws, Mobsters & Crooks: From the Old West to the Internet* were received from the following sources:

On the cover: Al Capone (**Archive Photos, Inc. Reproduced by permission**).

AP/Wide World Photos, Inc. Reproduced by permission: pp. 3, 11, 18, 31, 35, 45, 50, 56, 67, 72, 80, 87, 100, 109, 110, 127, 139, 151, 156, 159, 178, 186, 190, 193, 207, 217, 220, 226, 227, 230, 241, 247, 262, 266, 269, 270, 283, 305, 310, 311, 313, 328, 336, 351, 373, 392, 394, 437, 440, 443, 451, 459, 462; **Archive Photos, Inc. Reproduced by permission:** pp. 13, 21, 89, 121, 235, 292, 378, 410, 450; **UPI/Corbis-Bettmann. Reproduced by permission:** pp. 16, 22, 28, 41, 47, 54, 55, 58, 75, 93, 96, 105, 144, 147, 164, 177, 205, 261, 278, 294, 297, 325, 430, 434, 448, 456, 465; **Photograph by Greta Pratt. New York Times Co./Archive Photos, Inc. Reproduced by permission:** p. 39; **The Granger Collection, New York. Reproduced by permission:** pp. 113, 333, 355, 367, 387, 397, 412, 419, 492; **Popperfoto/Archive Photos, Inc. Reproduced by permission:** p. 133; **Photograph by Tammy Lechner. Los Angeles Times Photo. Reproduced by permission:** p. 189; **Reuters/The News and Observer-Jim/Archive Photos, Inc. Reproduced by permission:** p. 197; **Reuters/Corbis-Bettmann. Reproduced by permission:** p. 221; **Wyoming Division of Cultural Resources. Reproduced by permission:** p. 253; **Reuters/Jim Bourg/Archive Photos. Reproduced by permission:** p. 315; **Photograph by Eric Draper. AP/Wide World Photos, Inc. Reproduced by permission:** p. 317; **American Stock/Archive Photos, Inc. Reproduced by permission:** pp. 341, 347, 368; **The Library of Congress:** p. 360; **Corbis-Bettmann. Reproduced by permission:** pp. 364, 384, 398, 486, 490; **Corbis. Reproduced by permission:** pp. 380, 477, 482.

Mobsters

Extortion, election-fixing, and murder for hire. Gambling rackets and money laundering. Labor racketeering, narcotics trafficking, and prostitution. From the humble beginnings of pre-Prohibition era gangs to the latter-day nationally organized Mafia, mobsters of this century have transformed illegal opportunities into massive criminal operations.

In this section you'll be introduced to the Black Hand extortionists who preyed on Italian immigrants at the turn of the century, Al Capone's seemingly iron-clad criminal empire, the rise and fall of modern-day godfather John Gotti, and more. The mobsters' stories are filled with fierce loyalty and bitter betrayals, cunning schemes and brutal tactics—and few have happy endings.

Sam Battaglia

Born: 1908
Died: 1973

Sam "Teets" Battaglia rose from street crime to the top ranks of a criminal organization known as the Chicago Outfit before he received a prison sentence that ended his career. Over the course of forty years, he racked up more than two dozen arrests for assault, attempted murder, burglary, larceny, robbery, and extortion.

A STREET THUG ON THE RISE

Raised in Chicago, Illinois, Battaglia received very little education. He began a criminal record in 1924, at the age of sixteen, when he was arrested for burglary. During the late 1920s he joined the notorious 42 Gang, a loosely organized group of poor young street thugs. Among the 42 Gang's other members was **Sam Giancana** (see entry), who eventually rose to the top of the Mafia's Chicago Outfit.

Known as a crook with more brawn (muscle) than brains, Battaglia captured the attention of the general public—and other gangsters—when he pulled off a daring robbery on November 17, 1930. Using a gun, he robbed Mrs. William Hale Thompson—the governor's wife—of more than $15,000 in jewels. What's more, he pocketed the gun and badge of her chauffeur, who happened to be a Chicago policeman. Battaglia was arrested for the theft, but the case was eventually dropped. No witness was able to identify the gangster, who produced several witnesses to testify that they had seen him at the movies when the robbery was supposed to have taken place.

3

Taking the "Fifth"

Forced to testify in court or before senate committees, mobsters often cited the Fifth Amendment. The Fifth Amendment allows an individual to avoid presenting testimony that may be incriminating (testimony that proves their involvement in a crime). When Battaglia appeared before the McClellan Committee he reportedly "took the Fifth" sixty times. Some people claimed that Battaglia had not done so to avoid revealing his role in the mob's activities. Rather, they said he took the Fifth simply to avoid having to speak in public. He was afraid that his poor speech would make him look unintelligent.

MURDER, FRAUD, AND DRUGS

The mobsters in **Al Capone**'s (see entry) Chicago Outfit were impressed with Battaglia's bold approach. Throughout the 1930s he rose through the ranks of the Chicago syndicate (association). Battaglia oversaw the bulk of the mob's loansharking (illegal lending business) which charged unreasonably high interest for loans and used violence as a method to ensure payment. Acting as a sort of judge, Battaglia determined the fate of those who failed to repay their loans. Clients who were late in making payments were brought to a back room at a place called the Casa Madrid by Battaglia's lieutenants. There Battaglia decided his victim's penalty. Some got off lightly with harsh beatings. Others were killed.

By the 1950s Battaglia was also involved in extortion (obtaining money through force or intimidation), fraud, and murder. Working under former 42 gangster Sam Giancana, he became chief of the Chicago Outfit's narcotics (drugs) operations. As the head of this profitable arm of the mob's activities, Battaglia was responsible for selecting the gangsters who were allowed to traffic (deliver) drugs. Having reached one of the highest positions in the Chicago underworld, Battaglia became a wealthy man—a multi-millionaire who owned a retreat in the Illinois countryside and a lavish horse-breeding farm.

GIANCANA STEPS DOWN

By the middle of the 1960s, the reign of Sam Giancana as a Mafia leader was about to end. Hounded by the Federal Bureau of Investigation (FBI), his every move shadowed, he began to draw too much attention to the mob's activities. Paul Ricca and Tony Accardo, Giancana's Mafia superiors, asked him to step down from the top mob position in Chicago. A number of Chicago gangsters wanted the position for themselves—including Battaglia.

Battaglia was, to all appearances, next in the Mafia's chain of command. Giancana wanted Battaglia as his replacement. As

Chicago's 42 Gang

Possibly the worst youth gang ever to arise in an American city, the 42 Gang provided Al Capone's Chicago mob with many young recruits. Founded in 1925, the gang included members as young as nine years old. One of the gang's original leaders was Paul Battaglia, Sam's older brother.

Most of the 42's original members came from an area known as "the Patch"—an Italian section on the city's West Side. At constant war with the Chicago police, gang members held up nightclubs, robbed cigar stores, stripped cars, and stole from peddlers. They also killed the horses that pulled peddlers' carts, and sold their hind legs to businesses that purchased horse meat. In an incident that received a great deal of newspaper coverage, three gang members were caught casing the St. Charles boys' reformatory—where many gang members were serving sentences. The boys admitted that they were looking for a way for machine gunners to enter the reformatory in order to free their fellow gang members. The situation sparked a debate about the sentencing of juvenile criminals. Many people argued that toughened criminals such as 42 Gang members—even if they were children—deserved tougher sentences. *The Chicago Tribune,* for instance, claimed that 42ers deserved one of two sentences: Joliet penitentiary (prison) or the electric chair.

Initially, Capone's gang avoided using 42ers because they were considered to be too violent and unpredictable. Sam Giancana was reportedly the first 42er to be accepted into Capone's gang. A rising star in the underworld, Giancana brought a number of other 42ers into the mob—including Sam Battaglia, Charles Nicoletti, Sam DeStefano, Fifi Buccieri, Frank Caruso, Charles Nicoletti, Rocco Petenza, Marshall Caifano, Milwaukee Phil Alderisio, and Willie Daddano. The old 42 Gang companions who accompanied Giancana into the mob became known as the "Youngbloods." By the 1950s, the Youngbloods had become the foundation of the Chicago Outfit. Although they continued to take orders from the Mafia's old guard—which included Tony Accardo and Paul Ricca—the Youngbloods remained in power until Giancana was assassinated in 1975.

a former 42 gangster and loyal follower, he would be sure to allow the former leader to keep his hand in mob affairs. But in spite of Giancana's wishes, Ricca and Accardo appointed Joey Aiuppa, the head of Chicago's Cicero activities, and Jackie "the Lackey" Cerone, as joint heads of the Chicago Outfit. Battaglia might eventually have mounted a successful bid for the position had it not been for a conviction that resulted in a long imprison-

"Teets" Battaglia

How Battaglia received his nickname—"Teets"—has been the subject of debate. Some say he was so named because he had a well-developed, muscular chest. Others say it derived from his poor speech, or diction. When challenged by other mobsters, he supposedly threatened them by saying, "Shaddup or I'll bust ya in da teets [teeth]!"

ment. Found guilty of extortion, he was sentenced to fifteen years in prison—a term that proved to be a life sentence. Battaglia died in prison in 1973, after serving only six years of his sentence. He was sixty-five years old.

Sources for Further Reading

Sifakis, Carl. *The Mafia Encyclopedia.* New York: Facts on File, 1982, p. 30.

Who's Who in the Mafia. [Online] Available http://home1.pacific.net.sg/~seowjean/Mafia/mafia.html

The Black Hand Society

Active: 1890-1920

The Black Hand Society, a loose collection of Sicilian and Italian gangsters and freelancers, targeted communities across the United States where large numbers of Italian immigrants settled, extorting money from some of the wealthier people by threatening violence if the victim did not pay a fee.

LA MANO NERA

Prior to 1903, extortionists (people who obtain money through force or intimidation) signed their threatening letters with the names of Old World criminal societies, such as the Mafia (which was based in Sicily, an island south of Italy) and the Camorra (based in Naples, Italy). But that year, a case in which an extortionist signed his letters "La Mano Nera" received a great deal of publicity. A sensational story appeared in the *New York Herald,* and other newspapers followed. Soon many extortionists began to sign their letters with the fear-inspiring signature of the Black Hand. Both the press and the criminals themselves helped to create the impression that the Black Hand was an organized society of criminals. Many people eventually used the label—incorrectly—to refer to any violent crime that occurred in Italian neighborhoods in American cities. Although the Black Hand became associated with Italian crime, other national groups operated under the symbol as well.

The Society of the Black Hand

The real Society of the Black Hand was not Italian in origin. It began in Spain, during the Inquisition (a period when the Roman Catholic church sought out heretics, or nonbelievers), as a means to fight widespread oppression. The society eventually disappeared, but its name—*La Mano Nera* (the Black Hand)—lived on.

Mail fraud

For many years, the post office was the only government agency that managed to put a dent in Black Hand activity. Many Black Handers were prosecuted in federal courts on charges of mail fraud.

PAY OR DIE

The extortionist's method was simple. The victim—usually a prominent or wealthy member of the Italian or Sicilian American community—received a letter requesting that he pay a certain fee. The letter was "signed" by an imprint of a hand that had been dipped in black ink. The sender threatened violence if the victim did not pay. One Chicago Black Hander wrote:

> You got some cash. I need $1,000. You place the $100 bills in an envelope and place it underneath a board in the northeast corner of Sixty-ninth Street and Euclid Avenue at eleven o'clock tonight. If you place the money there, you will live. If you don't, you die. If you report this to the police, I'll kill you when I get out. They may save you the money, but they won't save you your life.

Most victims paid without question. Those who refused to pay were sometimes maimed (physically injured)—which gave them the chance to reconsider their refusal. Others were murdered, and sometimes entire families were killed. Black Hand victims were gunned down, knifed, poisoned, and hanged. Often, they were murdered in bomb explosions that killed innocent people in addition to the intended victims.

CHICAGO AND THE SHOTGUN MAN

The Black Hand business in Chicago began around 1890 and reached a peak around 1910 or 1911. Historians have estimated that about eighty unrelated gangs operated in the Black Hand business in Chicago at that time. Bombing was a common punishment for victims who refused to pay their extortionists. Officials estimated that during the thirty-year period from 1900 to 1930, eight hundred bombs had been targeted against Black Hand victims. Many of the bombings leveled entire buildings, killing the families of the intended victims as well as their neighbors. Among the Black Hand enforcers were Frank Campione, Sam Cardinelli, and a young man named Nicholas Viana, who was known as "The Choir Boy." The three, who had committed

Outlaws, Mobsters & Crooks

at least twenty bombings, were eventually hanged for murder.

Many Black Hand victims in Chicago were shot to death. And many were killed by the same hitman (person hired to kill). For several years during the peak of Black Hand activity in Chicago, between twelve and fifty victims were executed. One man, known simply as "the Shotgun Man," was reportedly responsible for one-third of those deaths. The hitman, whose identity was never discovered, was believed to have been a Sicilian who had operated as a Mafia assassin in his native country before settling in Chicago's Little Italy. In a seventy-two hour period in March of 1911, the Shotgun Man murdered four victims at the corner of Milton and Oak Streets—an intersection that became known as "Death Corner."

A tenor sings the blues

When Enrico Caruso, a famous opera tenor, received a Black Hand note demanding $2,000, he paid the fee. But when he received another threatening letter—asking for $15,000—he approached the police. After setting a trap, the police caught the thieves as they picked up the money from under the steps of a factory. The Black Handers were actually businessmen looking for easy money. (Many so-called Black Hand threats were actually made by businessmen who played on the public's fear of the mobsters.) Convicted of extortion, the two men were sentenced to prison.

Black Handers were rarely convicted and sent to prison. And Black Hand gangs wanted to keep it that way. Gangs often retaliated against victims who accused them. Because Caruso was responsible for the imprisonment of two extortionists, officials believed that his life was in danger. For the rest of his life, he was kept under police guard and private detective protection—both in the United States and in Europe.

The Shotgun Man terrorized Chicago for about eight or nine years. Paid well for his services, he enjoyed the protection of clients who had political ties. Few citizens had the courage to identify a Black Hand killer—especially one whose political ties would probably keep him out of jail. The Shotgun Man eventually disappeared from Chicago's Little Italy. Nothing is known about where he went next, and his true identity remains a mystery.

BLACK HANDS IN THE BIG APPLE

Like Chicago, New York first encountered Black Hand activity around 1890. Within ten years, the extortion racket had

Butcher in Brooklyn

In 1905 a wealthy Brooklyn butcher named Gaetano Costa received a Black Hand letter. It stated:

> You have more money than we have. We know of your wealth and that you are alone in this country. We want $1,000, which you are to put in a loaf of bread and hand to a man who comes in to buy meat and pulls out a red handkerchief.

Unlike most Black Hand targets, Costa refused to pay the fee. But his refusal did not go unpunished. Costa was shot to death behind the meat counter in his shop by Black Hand assassins. Although no one was ever charged with his murder, the hit men were known to work for "Lupo the Wolf," a Mafia gangster who terrorized Italian Harlem.

become a thriving business. In 1908 alone, 424 Black Hand cases were reported to the police. What's more, police estimated that for every case that was reported, another 250 were kept silent.

Ciro Terranova (who later became known as "the Artichoke King"), Johnny Torrio, and Frankie Uale (known as Yale) were among New York's Black Hand leaders. For thirty years, one of the most powerful Black Handers in the city was Ignazio Saietta—a man the newspapers called "Lupo the Wolf"—the leader of the Morellos, the most powerful Mafia crime family in New York at the turn of the century. The gang had ties to Palermo, Sicily, where it maintained contact with Mafia heads. The Morello family—which also had ties with gangs in Chicago and New Orleans—was involved in counterfeiting, kidnapping, murder, and extortion. As the leader of the gang, Saietta operated in the Italian Harlem district where many Sicilians lived. Although he openly practiced criminal activities, he managed to beat several indictments (charges of crimes), which earned him a reputation as an "untouchable"—someone who could not be touched by the law. He was feared by the Italian community—many of whom reportedly crossed themselves (asking God for protection) at the mention of his name.

It has been estimated that Saietta was responsible for about sixty Black Hand killings. Some were victims who refused to pay the extortion fee, while others were gangsters who threatened Saietta's territory. He was even responsible for the murder of a relative he suspected of having betrayed him. Many of the murders took place in a building at 323 East 107th Street in the heart of Italian Harlem. Victims were often tortured. Screams in the night were said to be commonplace at the site, which came to be known as the Murder Stable.

Eventually, police officials unearthed the remains of about sixty corpses on the grounds of Saietta's property.

Claiming that he was simply the building's landlord, Saietta
insisted that he could not be held responsible for the killings
that had taken place on the grounds. The supposed tenants
were Italians whose names could not be traced. No one was
ever convicted for the murders at the Murder Stable, and the
site continued to be used for murder and torture until about
1917.

Although Saietta was never convicted for his murderous activities in Italian Harlem, the Secret Service managed to peg him for operating a counterfeiting business in the Catskill Mountains in New York. Sentenced to thirty years in prison, he was paroled after ten years, in June of 1920.

NO WORK, SLIGHT RISK, VAST PAY

By 1920, Black Hand activity in the United States all but disappeared. The Saietta gang in New York had been broken up a decade earlier. Members of Chicago's Cardinella Black Hand gang were in prison or dead. And extortionists in Kansas City, Philadelphia, Pittsburgh, and San Francisco, were serving prison terms. Most were convicted of mail fraud—not of murder. Beginning in 1915, federal government officials began to enforce the laws that prohibit using the U.S. mail to defraud victims.

But successful prosecutions were only partly responsible for the decline of Black Hand activity. With the coming of Prohibition (when the Eighteenth Amendment outlawed the manufacture and sale of alcohol in the United States), many gangsters who had been involved in extortion turned to the much more profitable business of bootlegging. The illegal sale of liquor offered what writer Edward Dean Sullivan termed "No work—slight risk—vast remuneration [pay]." Soon the Black Hand—as a business and as a symbol—disappeared.

Sources for Further Reading

Nash, Jay Robert. *Bloodletters and Badmen.* New York: M. Evans, 1973, pp. 57–61.

Pitkin, Thomas. *The Black Hand: A Chapter in Ethnic Crime.* Lanham, MD: Rowman and Littlefield, 1977, pp. 1–14.

Sifakis, Carl. *The Mafia Encyclopedia.* New York: Facts on File, 1982, pp.l 36–38.

Al Capone

Born: 1899
Died: January 25, 1947
AKA: "Scarface"

Like many of his associates, Al Capone rose from the ranks of poor street thugs to the upper level of Chicago's underworld. As one of the nation's most powerful mobsters, he seemed untouchable—until the government charged him with tax fraud as a means to put him in prison.

SCARFACE

Born on January 17, 1899, Alphonse Capone was the fourth of nine children. His parents immigrated from Naples, Italy, and settled in New York. Raised in the tough Williamsburg section of Brooklyn, Capone left school after the sixth grade after becoming involved in a fight with one of his teachers. He never returned to school.

At a young age, Capone became involved with small-time street criminals operating in his neighborhood. As a member of the James Street Gang, he became close friends with the gang's leader, Johnny Torrio. The two remained lifelong friends, as did Capone and Lucky Luciano, who later became one of the most prominent criminals in the country.

Capone eventually graduated to the James Street mob's senior gang, the Five Points gang. Still in his teens, he worked as a gunman for the notorious New York gang. Torrio and his partner, Frankie Uale (known as Yale), employed Capone as a bouncer at a Brooklyn saloon. There Capone got into a brawl in

Scarface

Capone was known as "Scarface" because he bore three jagged scars on his left cheek. Although the scars were the remnants of a bar fight, Capone often told reporters that he received his wounds serving in France in the "Lost Battalion" during World War I (1914-1918). Capone never served in the Lost Battalion—or any other regiment—during any war.

which he was slashed on the cheek with a razor. The incident left the gangster with an unsightly scar—three jagged marks that remained pale and hairless—on his left cheek. The incident earned him the lifelong nickname of "Scarface."

BIG JIM AND THE WINDY CITY

In 1919, Capone moved to Chicago to escape arrest on a murder charge. Already settled in Chicago was Torrio, who had come to help his uncle, Big Jim Colosimo, run his far-reaching prostitution operations. Capone arrived in Chicago the same year the U.S. Congress declared the ratification (approval) of the Eighteenth Amendment, which outlawed the manufacture, sale, and transport of alcoholic beverages nationwide. Almost overnight, scores of Chicago gangsters turned their attention to the profitable business of bootlegging.

Working for Colosimo's organization, Capone started as a bouncer at one of the gangster's businesses. He later worked as a bagman (collecting payments) and enforcer, for which he was handsomely paid. In 1920, Colosimo was assassinated in what is considered to be Chicago's first gangland hit. Many assumed that Capone and Torrio had planned the murder in order to take over the mobster's rackets. Both had alibis—proof that they were elsewhere when the crime was committed.

AN EMPIRE SOUTH OF MADISON

With Colosimo out of the way, Torrio took control of one of the largest crime empires in America. An intelligent businessman, Torrio turned the organization's bootlegging activities into a multi-million dollar operation. Through a series of efficient murders, Capone became Torrio's top lieutenant. The Torrio-Capone gang expanded its influence throughout much of the city, taking over less powerful mobs and waging war with rival organizations.

Madison Street, in downtown Chicago, provided the dividing line between the city's two most powerful gangs. It separat-

Eliot Ness and the Untouchables

In 1928, when he was placed in charge of a Prohibition enforcement team created to bring down Capone, Eliot Ness (1902–1957) was just twenty-six years old. Ness examined hundreds of files of Prohibition agents before he selected the nine men who would make up his squad. He selected the agents for their clean records and loyalty to the cause. In time the agents became known as the Untouchables—because they could not be touched by bribery or threats of violence. Ness's agents—all of whom were in their twenties—were specialists in various activities, including the use of weapons and wiretapping.

Ness and his team of Untouchables attempted to ruin Capone by conducting regular raids of the gangster's illegal stills (apperatuses used to make alcohol) and other bootlegging operations. While these efforts hurt Capone financially, they did not succeed in dismantling his criminal empire. As Ness's team harassed Capone's organization, other federal agents focused on gathering evidence of tax evasion—evidence that would finally remove Capone from Chicago's underworld operations.

Although Ness is best recognized for his work with the Untouchables in Chicago, his career extended far beyond the Prohibition era. In 1935, he was hired by the reform mayor of Cleveland to investigate the racketeers who had placed a stronghold on the city's commercial activity. Ness introduced a program to reform the police force, attacking bribery and graft (to gain money by dishonest means) in the department and reducing crime by an estimated 25 percent. During the next three years a combination of surveillance and undercover work resulted in the destruction of Cleveland's Mayfield Road Mob, a violent gang of Italian and Jewish criminals.

Ness left his position in Cleveland to serve as the federal director of the Division of Social Protection for the Office of Defense during World War II (1939–1945). In peacetime, he became a private businessman. He died in 1957, at the age of fifty-seven.

ed the Capone-Torrio South Side territory from Charles Dion O'Banion's North Side empire. For the most part, the two rival organizations respected the territorial boundary—although Capone was eager to establish prostitution in the brothel-free North Side.

SCARFACE TAKES OVER

Three Capone gunmen walked into O'Banion's North Side flower shop on November 8, 1924, under the pretense of buying

Eliot Ness.

flowers for a funeral. As one shook O'Banion's hand, the two others shot him dead.

It was not long before O'Banion gangsters struck back. On January 24, 1925, Torrio was ambushed by mobsters from the North Side gang. He was shot several times in the stomach, chest, arm, and jaw. Next, **Bugs Moran** (see entry) put a gun to his head. The gun jammed and the would-be assassins fled. Critically wounded, Torrio was near death for days. Released from the hospital the following month, Torrio announced his decision to leave Chicago's rackets. Just twenty-six years old at the time, Capone stepped in to take his place.

VOTER PERSUASION

Although other bootleggers operated in Chicago during the 1920s, Capone was more ruthless, greedy, shrewd, and systematic than the rest. He was suspected of being behind nearly two hundred killings in Chicago during the decade. To carry out his assassinations, he employed such notorious gunmen as Frank "the Enforcer" Nitti, August "Augie Dogs" Pisano, and Louis "Luigi" Morganno. He also managed to achieve working relationships with various powerful Chicago politicians, particularly Mayor William "Big Bill" Thompson.

Capone often bragged that he "owned" Chicago. To ensure that the politicians who were friendly to his organization remained in power, Capone controlled the outcome of many local elections. He sent gangs of thugs to the election polls (a place where votes are cast or recorded). Brandishing guns and other weapons, Capone's gangsters bullied voters into casting their ballot for the Capone candidate. Those who did not cooperate were often beaten, kidnapped, or shot dead.

A NEAR-DEATH EXPERIENCE AT THE HAWTHORNE INN

Capone's role as a top player in the Chicago underworld was not without risks. He was constantly pursued by would-be assas-

The Saint Valentine's Day massacre

By early 1929, Capone had neutralized most of his major underworld enemies in Chicago. But one gang operating on the North Side, led by Bugs Moran, continued to challenge him. Capone decided to do away with the gang's leadership—and Moran, in particular. Through informants, Capone knew that Moran's gang gathered regularly in a garage on North Clark Street to await the arrival of their liquor-truck convoys. And he knew that one such shipment was due to arrive at 10:30 A.M. on February 14, 1929—St. Valentine's Day. Capone ordered his main enforcer, Fred "Killer" Burke, to prepare a surprise for Moran and company.

sins—one of whom attempted to poison his soup. One of the most notorious attempts on Capone's life occurred in 1926. The North Side O'Banion gang—which had been responsible for the attempt on Torrio's life—staged a massive ambush at Capone's headquarters at the Hawthorne Inn, on the West Side of the city.

On September 20, in broad daylight, several cars stopped in front of the Capone headquarters. North Side gunmen fired into the first floor of the hotel and surrounding shops—all of which were owned by Capone's organization. Capone's headquarters was riddled with bullet holes from shotgun, revolver, and machine-gun fire. Capone—who had been thrown to the floor by his bodyguard, Frank Rio—was unharmed.

A BLOODBATH, BRIBERY, AND LIFE BEHIND BARS

In the months and years following the Hawthorne Inn shootout, a number of Capone's rivals disappeared. **Hymie Weiss** (see entry), who had taken part in the shooting, was gunned down in front of O'Banion's North Side flower shop by Capone hitmen, Albert Anselmi and John Scalise. Vincent "the Schemer" Drucci, another North Sider who participated in the ambush, died at the hands of a policeman. **Two Gun Alterie** (see entry) left town, leaving Moran as the head of what remained of the North Side O'Banion gang. In February 1929, in an attempt to kill Moran, Capone ordered an ambush. The shooting, known as the "Saint Valentine's Day

Al Capone's
bullet-proof car.

Massacre," killed seven O'Banion gangsters. But Moran was not among them.

It was decided that three gunmen would gain access to the garage by disguising themselves as Chicago police officers conducting a routine raid. Through cash payoffs, Capone laid hold of a police car and several police uniforms. Since the intended victims already knew most of the Capone mob, members of the **Purple Gang** (see entry) from Detroit, Michigan, were hired to pose as the policemen.

When the disguised men entered the garage, they encountered seven men: Pete and Frank Gusenberg (Moran's most dangerous gunmen), Adam Heyer (reputed to be the bookkeeper for the gang), Albert Kashellek (Moran's brother-in-law), John

May and Reinhart Schwimmer (both minor gang figures), and Albert Weinshank (a speakeasy operator who bore a striking physical resemblance to Moran).

Mistaking Weinshank for Moran, who was having coffee in a diner three blocks away, the phony policemen ordered all seven to raise their hands and stand facing the back wall. At that point, Burke and a companion quietly entered the garage, and the hit team opened fire on the men with three machine guns, a shotgun, and a revolver. Within thirty seconds the seven lay dead on the floor. Two innocent bystanders were also killed. Leaving the floor strewn with two hundred spent cartridges, the killers drove away in the police car. None of the guilty parties were ever prosecuted for their role in the "Saint Valentine's Day Massacre." Capone, who was in Florida at the time, had an airtight alibi (proof that he was elsewhere).

Law officers were never able to prove that Capone was directly involved in any of the murders he planned—including the bloody Saint Valentine's Day massacre. But the previous year, after extensive investigation, U.S. Treasury agents uncovered evidence that Capone had never filed income tax returns on his vast earnings. In June of 1931, the gangster was formally charged with income tax evasion. Although he reportedly offered authorities a $4 million bribe, he was tried in October of that year. Before the trial ended, the original jury had to be replaced; Capone had bribed them.

Convicted in October 1931, Capone was sentenced to eleven years imprisonment at hard labor, which he served at a federal penitentiary in Atlanta, Georgia, and at Alcatraz (also known as "the Rock"), located in San Francisco Bay, California. During this long period in prison he lost all his power within American organized crime. Released on parole November 19, 1939, Capone suffered from paresis of the brain. (Paresis is a form of paralysis. It was probably brought on by untreated syphilis, a sexually transmitted disease he had contracted as a young man.) He retired to his mansion in Palm Island, Florida, where he died on January 25, 1947.

Savage Al

Capone refused to tolerate betrayal. On May 7, 1929, he threw a banquet in honor of three of his top gunmen, Albert Anselmi, Joseph "Hop Toad" Giunta, and John Scalise. The three killers attended, unaware that Capone had discovered they were plotting against him. Before the evening was over, Capone clubbed the three men to death in front of his horrified dinner guests.

Sources for Further Reading

Nash, Jay Robert. *Bloodletters and Badmen.* New York: M. Evans, 1973, pp. 97–105.

Sifakis, Carl. *The Mafia Encyclopedia.* New York: Facts on File, 1982, pp. 60–62.

Vandome, Nick. *Crimes and Criminals.* New York: Chambers, 1992, pp. 54–56.

Carlo Gambino

Born: September 1, 1902
Died: October 15, 1975

Carlo Gambino ruled the most powerful Mafia family in the United States. Unlike the majority of other Mafia bosses, whose careers were cut short by rivals and law enforcement officials, Gambino seemed to be unthreatened by his enemies—and by the government that attempted to curtail the Mafia's activities.

THE ROAD TO *SOTOCAPO*

Carlo Gambino was born in Palermo, Sicily, in a section that was so thoroughly controlled by the Mafia that police reportedly would not visit the area. As a teenager he traveled to America as a stowaway on a ship called the S.S. *Vincenzo Florila*. After arriving in Newport, Virginia, on December 23, 1921, Gambino made his way to Brooklyn, New York, where a number of close relatives lived. Living in a small apartment on Navy Street, he went to work for a small trucking company owned by his uncle. Gambino married Kathryn Castellano, his first cousin.

Together with his two brothers-in-law—Paul and Peter Castellano—and Thomas Masotto, a first cousin, Gambino joined New York's Mafia organization. At the time of his initiation into the family, Gambino worked for Joseph Masseria—known as "Joe the Boss." Soon after, Masseria was assassinated on the orders of a rival Mafia chief Salvatore Maranzano. The bloody ambush was carried out by Nick Capuzzi, Joe Profaci, Joe Valachi, and a Chicago gunman known simply as "Buster."

THE CARLO GAMBINO FAMILY

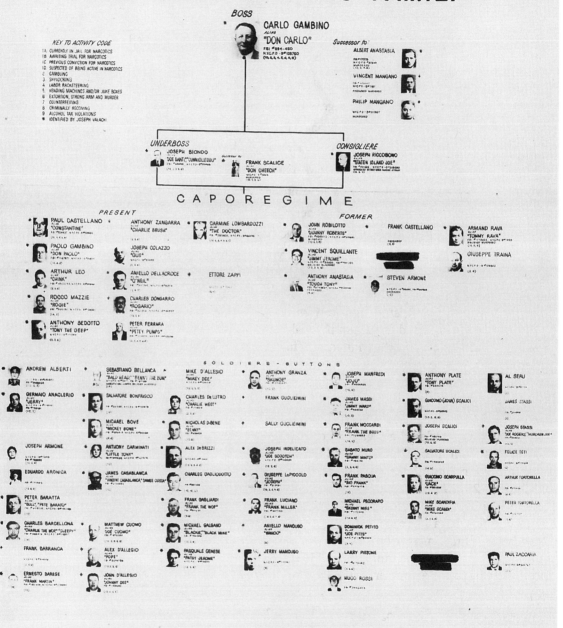

| Outlaws, Mobsters & Crooks

With Masseria dead, Gambino shifted his loyalty to Maranzano. But Maranzano's time as a Mafia boss was short-lived: he was killed in 1931 by associates of Lucky Luciano.

After Luciano divided the New York Mafia into five "families," Gambino and his cousins joined forces with the family of Vincent Mangano. The Mangano family ran a number of rackets in Brooklyn, including horse betting, the numbers (another form of betting), and the Italian lottery. The Manganos' reign lasted until 1951, when Phil Mangano was murdered by hitmen under Albert Anastasia. At about the same time, Vincent Mangano disappeared. His body was never found. Anastasia took over as the head of the family, making Gambino—who reportedly played a role in the Mangano affair—his *sotocapo,* or underboss.

A grave situation

At one point, Gambino was on the hit list of fellow New York Mafia boss Joe Bonanno. A treacherous gangster, Bonanno plotted to kill at least three other Mafia bosses before Gambino convinced him to leave New York in exchange for control of the rackets in California.

Bonanno has been given credit for an unusual solution to an age-old Mafia problem: the disposal of the corpses of murdered victims. He is said to have invented the split-level coffin. The victim's body was taken to a Brooklyn funeral home where it was placed in the lower compartment of a coffin. The top compartment contained another body. The two corpses were buried together in a legitimate (lawful) ceremony. Buried in someone else's grave, the victims were safely beyond the reach of inquisitive detectives and police.

ANASTASIA

Anastasia expanded the organization to include new rackets, such as loan-sharking, gambling, and narcotics trafficking. But Gambino was not content to remain an underboss in the Mafia. On October 25, 1957, Anastasia was shot to death as he sat in a barber's chair in Manhattan's Park-Sheraton Hotel. The assassins struck when Anastasia's face was wrapped in hot towels—after his bodyguards had mysteriously disappeared. Historians believe that Gambino and another gangster, Vito Genovese, were responsible for arranging the murder. According to Joe Valachi, a mem-

Opposite page: The Carlo Gambino "family" chart, shown at a Senate crime inquiry on October 8, 1963, during the testimony of Mafia informant Joe Valachi.

ber of the Mafia who later became an informant, Gambino had arranged the hit with the approval of other Mafia bosses. "He had a good excuse," Valachi told officials. "Albert was losing at the track [betting on horses], he was there every day, and was abusing people more than ever on account of that."

With Anastasia out of the way, and other Mafia bosses on his side, Gambino set his sights on ruling the family. Together with Luciano and two other bosses—**Frank Costello** (see entry) and **Meyer Lansky** (see entry)—he plotted Genovese's downfall. Genovese had helped arrange Anastasia's murder in hopes of taking over his position. But before he was able to stake a claim to the business, Gambino and his three associates set him up to be convicted in a narcotics case. Captured by federal agents, Genovese was tried and sentenced to fifteen years in prison. He died in prison before the end of his term.

CARLO AND THE LITTLE LAMB

The position Gambino assumed was that of the strongest family boss in New York. But his right to the position was not undisputed. Aniello Dellacroce, who had been a loyal supporter of Anastasia, wanted a piece of the business for himself. A smart leader, Gambino managed to win Dellacroce over. Before discussions began, Dellacroce's closest associate, Armand Rava, disappeared. Then Gambino invited Dellacroce to a meeting, where he offered to make him the family's *sotocapo*. Dellacroce accepted.

Gambino assigned the violent portion of his business to Dellacroce. Loan-sharking and extortion both relied on violence, or the threat of violence—something that Dellacroce excelled at. As Gambino's underboss, he earned a ruthless reputation even among Mafia hitmen. Dellacroce—whose full name translates as "Little Lamb of the Cross"—apparently enjoyed violence. A federal official once said of him, "He likes to peer into a victim's face, like some kind of dark angel, at the moment of death."

With Dellacroce in charge of the dirty work, Gambino was able to concentrate on other more profitable areas of business. He devoted his efforts to illegal rackets—such as fixing the price of construction bids, setting up dishonest connections in the labor unions, and creating a monopoly (exclusive control) in garbage collection. He also participated in gambling, hijacking, and narcotics ventures, and became involved in legal businesses that drew on Mafia manpower to threaten competitors. Made up of about one thousand men, Gambino's family had operations that extended from western Massachusetts to the far reaches of Philadelphia, Pennsylvania.

THE BOSS OF BOSSES

At the height of his power, Gambino headed what law enforcement officials described as the largest, richest, and strongest Mafia family in the United States. During his reign as Mafia chieftain, a number of other Mafia bosses toppled from their positions. Joseph Bonanno, the boss of another New York family, was forced into retirement after a failed challenge to Gambino's power. Joseph Colombo, another New York family boss, was shot at a rally after he angered Gambino with behavior that brought too much public attention to Mafia activities. Colombo's murderer was killed at the scene by an unknown shooter. Gambino also exercised a great deal of power over the four other New York Mafia families, and he played a key role in the national commission that determined the guidelines for all Mafia families in the United States. The single most powerful boss in New York's underworld, Gambino became known as the *capo di tutti capi*—the boss of bosses.

A soft-spoken man, Gambino had what has been described as a courtly (elegant and polite) manner. Joseph Catalupo, a government informer, described him as "very even-tempered, very polite, very much the gentleman in the presence of others." A strong family man, he lived on the upper floor of a two-family home in Brooklyn with his wife and children. He eventually bought a modest waterfront home in Massapequa, on Long Island, New York. An exceptionally wealthy man, he never attracted attention by assuming the lifestyle of the rich and famous. He dressed simply and was driven around New York in an inexpensive car.

POOR HEALTH

By the middle of the 1960s, Gambino received a constant flurry of legal summonses called subpoenas (pronounced suh-PEE-nas) to appear before the grand jury. He managed to avoid appearing in court thanks to lawyers who filed medical documents proving that his health was poor. Gambino's poor health also helped him avoid deportation (a forced return to his native country). Having entered the country as a stowaway, Gambino was considered to be an illegal alien. In 1970, the U.S. Supreme Court upheld an earlier order of deportation. When government officials attempted to carry out the order, Gambino was taken to the hospital. His family announced that the Mafia leader had suffered a heart attack— just in time to avoid deportation. Although the attack looked suspicious, government doctors determined that Gambino had, in fact, suffered a serious heart attack.

Gambino died of a heart attack five years later in his home on Long Island. Following his death, rumors circulated that another Mafia boss—Carmine Galente, whose nickname was "the Cigar"—had ordered his spies to convince Gambino to take a swine-flu shot. Such a shot could have endangered the health of a weak, elderly man with a bad heart. According to federal officials, Gambino received a flu shot shortly before he died. Gambino's role of mob boss was taken over by his brother-in-law, Paul Castellano.

Sources for Further Reading

"After the Don: A Donnybrook?" *Time* (November 1, 1976), p. 39.

"Carlo Gambino." *The New York Times Obituaries* (October 16, 1975), p. 26.

Jackson, Kenneth T., ed. *Dictionary of American Biography.* Supplement 10. New York: Simon & Schuster Macmillan, 1976-1980, pp. 268–270.

Sifakis, Carl. *The Mafia Encyclopedia.* New York: Facts on File, 1982, pp. 131–132.

Sam Giancana

Born: May 24, 1908
Died: June 19, 1975

Sam Giancana is believed to have been responsible for hundreds of mob-related murders. He entered the Mafia as a Youngblood—a new breed of young criminals who started out in Chicago's notorious 42 Gang—and worked his way up to head the mob's Chicago Outfit.

A TOUGH YOUNG THUG

Gilormo Giancana was born on the West side of Chicago in 1908. Baptized Momo Salvatore Giancana, he was known as "Sam." He lived with his parents—Antonino Giancana, a Sicilian immigrant grocer, and Antonia DiSimone—in a tenement (a housing structure for the poor) on South Aberdeen Street in a neighborhood referred to as "The Patch." A grade-school dropout, Giancana became involved in a violent gang of youths called "the 42s." One of the worst juvenile gangs in Chicago in the 1920s, the 42 Gang was often employed by more older, more powerful gangsters to carry out beatings, getaways, and other gang-related activities. By his late teens, Giancana was the head of the 42s and had become a well-respected "wheelman," or driver, for more established gangsters. He soon graduated to the position of "triggerman"—a role that called for a ruthless willingness to kill.

Giancana was first arrested and convicted at the age of eighteen for auto theft. He was also indicted (formally charged) for murder at the age of eighteen, although he was never tried. The key witness for the prosecution was killed before the matter went to trial. By the time Giancana was twenty he had been arrested as the prime suspect in three murder investigations. One of the murder victims was an African American man who had been running for committeeman in the Twentieth Ward—an area that was predominantly Italian.

MOVING UP

Giancana first worked for the "Chicago Outfit"—the Chicago arm of the Mafia—as a chauffeur and getaway driver for Paul "The Waiter" Ricca. As Ricca's protégé (someone who is trained by a person with more experience), he quickly moved up through the ranks of the Chicago Mafia. On September 26, 1933, he married Angeline DeTolve; they had three daughters together.

Convicted of moonshining (manufacturing alcohol illegally) in 1939, Giancana was sentenced to four years in prison. There he met Edward Jones, who ruled the South Side's numbers racket (illegal gambling). Giancana learned all that he could about the illegal lottery gambling operation. When he was released from prison, he set out with other former members of the 42 Gang to take over the numbers operations in Chicago's African American neighborhoods. Following a series of beatings, kidnappings, and murders, he won control of the numbers racket, which increased the income of the Chicago Outfit by millions of dollars each year.

Friends in high places

Giancana was at one time a friend to singer Frank Sinatra. The subject of nonstop surveillance by the FBI, Giancana asked him for help. Frank Sinatra, a popular singer and actor, was at one time a good friend of both the mobster and President John Kennedy. Giancana hoped that Sinatra would be able to use his friendship with the president to influence the Justice Department. One of Giancana's associates reported to him (in a wiretap intercepted by the FBI in December 1961):

I had a chance to quiz [Sinatra]. He says, "Johnny, I took Sam's name and wrote it down and told Bobby Kennedy [the president's brother, who, as the attorney general, had declared war on the mob] this is my buddy. This is my buddy, this is what I want you to know, Bob."

But Sinatra was not successful. Giancana later complained that Sinatra could not "get change for a quarter" from the Kennedys. He was so angry, in fact, that later wiretaps revealed that he discussed whether to "hit" Sinatra and some of his friends for failing to act on his behalf.

During World War II, Giancana avoided serving in the military by telling the truth. Asked what he did for a living, he replied "I steal." He was declared 4F (unfit for service) after a Selective Service officer (person who drafts people for military service) concluded that he was a "constitutional psychopath [someone with an aggressive personality disorder] with an inadequate personality manifested by strong antisocial trends." Giancana spent the war years operating a number of illegal rackets, including forging rationing stamps. (Rationing stamps were used during the war to distribute limited items such as sugar.) When Ricca went to prison in 1944, Giancana became the driver for Anthony "Tough Tony" Accardo, the next gangster in the mob's line of command. By 1945 Giancana had moved with his family to the wealthy Chicago suburb of Oak Park.

THE NEW MAFIA

By the 1950s, Anthony Accardo began to back away from heading the Chicago Outfit's operations. Many members of the old guard—mobsters who had worked for **Al Capone** (see entry)—were old, retired, imprisoned, or dead. With Accardo and Ricca's backing, Giancana became the head of the mob's Chicago operations. He took with him many of his former 42 Gang associates, who became known as the Mafia's Young Turks or Youngbloods.

By 1955 Giancana presided over 1,500 Mafiosi (members of the Mafia) in three states. He oversaw operations that included gambling, prostitution, loan sharking, narcotics trafficking, and other illegal activities. As a prominent figure in the "New Mafia," he took part in the corruption of labor unions and had interests in gambling casinos and legitimate businesses. Branching into new operations, the Chicago Outfit relied increasingly on dishonest police and corrupt politicians. Under Giancana's supervision, the Chicago Mafia evolved from a relatively small-time neighborhood racket into a large-scale criminal organization.

A BUG IN THE BACKROOM

Giancana's position at the head of the Chicago Outfit was short lived. In 1959 his career took a downturn after FBI agents planted a microphone in the backroom of the Armory Lounge in the suburb of Forest Park—the headquarters of Giancana's operation. With the listening device hidden among cans of olive oil and tomato paste, federal agents eavesdropped on the mobsters' conversations for six years. The bugging provided the FBI with intimate knowledge of the mob's activities in Chicago and elsewhere.

In 1965—after he refused to testify about the Mob's activities before a federal grand jury in Chicago—Giancana was sentenced to one year in prison. When he was released he left the

Sam Giancana's home in Oak Park, Illinois. Giancana was found shot to death in the basement on June 20, 1975.

United States to avoid further questioning. Living in an estate near Cuernavaca, Mexico, he avoided U.S. federal authorities until 1974—when the Mexican government forced him to leave the country, giving him no explanation for the expulsion.

When Giancana returned to Chicago, he was no longer a major player in the Mafia. Forced out of the boss's position, he was replaced by Joey Aiuppa—a situation that thoroughly displeased him. Granted immunity (protection) from further prosecution, Giancana appeared four times before the federal grand jury. During his final appearance, in February of 1975, he was questioned about mob activities in Latin America. He reportedly said little to shed light on the Mafia's activities. Giancana was next scheduled to testify in Washington before a Senate committee that was investigating the Mafia's involvement in a Central Intelligence Agency (CIA) plot to assassinate Cuban leader Fidel Castro.

THE LAST SUPPER

On June 19, 1975—having recently returned from Houston, Texas, where he underwent a gall bladder operation—Giancana invited a number of trusted friends to his Oak Park home to celebrate his homecoming. He invited only his closest friends and family, including one of his daughters and her husband, his driver, Dominick "Butch" Blazi, and Charles "Chuckie" English, a partner in many of his mob activities. The party—which took place days before Giancana was to appear in Washington—was watched by FBI agents who were interested in seeing who the mobster's associates were.

Sometime after his guests had left, Giancana went into a basement kitchen to cook Italian sausages and spinach for himself—and possibly someone else. But the meal went untouched. Shortly after 11 P.M. Giancana's housekeeper went to the basement to check on him. He found the mobster on the kitchen floor, lying face up in a pool of blood. Giancana had been shot seven times in the face and neck.

A PUZZLING MURDER

On the surface, the murder looked like a gang execution. Standing inches from his victim, using a silencer on an automatic weapon, Giancana's killer first shot him once in the back of the head. Then he rolled him over to fire six more bullets from beneath his chin up into his jaw and brain. (Since a single bullet in the head is not always deadly, hired assassins fire multiple shots into their victims.) There were no signs of struggle. Giancana was found with a money clip containing $1,400 in his pants pocket—ruling out robbery as a motive for the killing. Apart from some shell casings, the killer left no clues. And after the murder, the Mafia's head boss, **Carlo Gambino** (see entry), reportedly ordered a contract on the killer—a typical precaution to cover up all traces of involvement following Mafia executions.

But a few things about Giancana's killing caused officials to question whether it really was a mob hit. Giancana was shot with a .22-caliber weapon—unlike the heavy guns usually chosen by Mafia hitmen. And Giancana had been shot in the back of the head—not the sort of "respectful" execution that a former Mafia boss should receive, according to the mob's code of honor.

A number of theories circulated about who had killed Giancana. The CIA might have wanted his role in the Castro plot kept quiet—but CIA director William Colby declared his agency had nothing to do with the killing. The Chicago Crime Commission came up with three reasons why other mob heads might have wanted him dead. Giancana might have tried to muscle his way back into power in Chicago rackets; he might have cheated other bosses by keeping all the profits from his Latin American operations; and they might have been afraid of what he would reveal at his upcoming hearing before the Senate committee. But Mafia heads publicly denied any involvement in Giancana's murder. Some people speculated that the onetime Chicago boss had been shot down by a former girlfriend—of whom he had many. No one was ever arrested for Giancana's murder.

> **Take a look at this!**
>
> *Hoodlum* (1996) tells the story of the 1930s Harlem gang war in which "Bumpy" Johnson, Dutch Schultz (played by Tim Roth in an over-the-top performance), and Lucky Luciano (played by Andy Garcia) battled for control of the area's numbers racket.

> **Career criminal**
>
> Giancana was once detained by an FBI agent in an airport. When the agent asked what he did for a living, Giancana responded, "Easy. I own Chicago. I own Miami. I own Las Vegas."

Sources for Further Reading

Brownstein, Ronald. *The Power and the Glitter.* New York: Pantheon Books, 1990, pp. 152–167.

"The Demise of a Don." *Time* (June 30, 1975), p. 26.

"Giancana, Gangster, Slain." *The New York Times* (June 21, 1975), pp. 11–12.

Jackson, Kenneth T. *Dictionary of American Biography.* Supplement 9. New York: Charles Scribner's Sons, 1971–1975, pp. 306–307.

Sifakis, Carl. *The Mafia Encyclopedia.* New York: Facts on File, 1982, pp. 138–140.

John Gotti

Born: October 27, 1940

John Gotti graduated from a youth gang and moved quickly through the ranks of the Mafia. Fond of wearing $1,800 suits and hand-painted ties, he became a powerful don (Mafia leader) at a relatively young age. He seemed immune to the government's attempts to convict him—until a close associate betrayed him.

ROUGH, TOUGH, AND DIRT POOR

Named after his father, John Joseph Gotti was born in the Bronx in New York on October 27, 1940. The son of a construction worker, he had five brothers. The Gotti family moved to Sheepshead Bay, Brooklyn, when John was in the fourth grade. Already street tough, Gotti and his brothers held their own against the neighborhood's reigning hoodlums, the Santoro brothers. A bright student, Gotti attended P.S. (Public School) 209 through the end of the sixth grade.

When Gotti was twelve his family moved to Brownsville-East, New York. The area supported a thriving underworld (Mafia activity). The breeding ground for the mob's hit squad called Murder, Inc., it was the former stomping ground of gangsters such as **Bugsy Siegel** (see entry) and "Kid Twist" Reles. Gotti attended P.S. 178 and, together with his friend Angelo Ruggiero, joined a gang known as the Fulton-Rockaway Boys. Soon recognized as a bright and tough opponent, he fought members of rival gangs such as the Liberty Park Tots and New

Lots Boys. Gotti's public school education ended on June 7, 1954, when he was suspended from the eighth grade. He never returned to school.

IN AND OUT OF JAIL

Even as a teenager, Gotti was confident and self-assured—attributes that attracted the notice of the neighborhood's older gangsters. Gotti's adult criminal record began at the age of eighteen, when he was picked up for frequenting a gambling location. A favorite pupil of the local Mafia heads, Carmine and Danny Fatico, Gotti also made a favorable impression on the mob's Gambino family before he was twenty years old.

In 1960, Gotti married Victoria DiGiorgio, the daughter of an Italian construction contractor and a Russian-Jewish woman. The couple eventually settled in Queens, in Howard Beach-Ozone Park, a blue-collar Italian-American neighborhood. Still a young struggling petty criminal, Gotti was arrested in January 1965 for bookmaking and again, two months later, for attempted burglary. (A bookmaker, or bookie, is someone who accepts and pays off bets.) He spent one year in jail. He was arrested again in December 1967 for stealing a truckload of electrical equipment and clothing from Kennedy airport in New York—and again, the following month, for the same offense. When he was released after serving three years in prison, Gotti moved in to replace the Fatico brothers, who were stepping down as the neighborhood mob leaders. Soon he was reporting to Aniello Dellacroce, Angelo Ruggiero's uncle, a powerful underboss in the Mob's Gambino family.

A MADE MAN

On May 22, 1973, a man named James McBratney was killed by three men in Snoopy's Bar in Staten Island, New York. The reason for McBratney's murder has been the subject of debate. The killing might have been payback for a number of thefts for which McBratney was responsible. And it might have been intended as punishment for his supposed role in the kidnapping and murder of Manny Gambino, the nephew of Mafia boss **Carlo Gambino** (see entry).

Although most of the seven witnesses claimed not to have seen the McBratney murder, the killers were finally identified as Angelo Ruggiero, Ralphie "the Wig" Galione, and John Gotti. More than two years later, on June 2, 1975, Gotti pleaded guilty to attempted manslaughter in the second degree, for which he was sentenced to four years in prison. Paroled (released from prison early) a little more than two years later, Gotti returned home on July 28, 1977.

The McBratney killing had helped Gotti move up within the Mafia. Soon after his release from prison he was formally initiated into the Mafia to become what is known as a "made man." He continued to report to Dellacroce, the Gambino family underboss. But he began to express dissatisfaction with the chain of command. Carlo Gambino, the mob's overall boss, had been replaced by Gambino's brother-in-law, "Big Paul" Castellano. Gotti disliked Castellano, and felt that Dellacroce was more deserving of the position of overall boss.

Bad memory

Three men approached John Favara as he walked to his car after work in Hyde Park, Long Island. One hit him with a board, while the others pushed him into a van. The owner of a nearby diner saw the incident. A couple of days later, the three men arrived at the diner. They drank coffee and said nothing. And they stared at the diner owner—who suddenly developed a memory problem that prevented him from identifying Favara's kidnappers.

UNNEIGHBORLY BEHAVIOR

On March 18, 1980, Gotti's neighbor, a fifty-one-year-old factory worker named John Favara, headed to his home in Howard Beach. As he drove down 157th Avenue, he was blinded by the sun. He never saw Frank Gotti, John Gotti's youngest son, pull into the street on a motor bike. Favara struck and killed the twelve-year-old boy.

Taking the advice of a priest he consulted, Favara did not attend Frankie's funeral. Nor did he contact Frankie's parents to offer his sympathy. Within days of the accident, Favara began to receive threats against his life. He ignored the warnings and continued about his business, working a regular shift at the Castro Convertible factory on Long Island. And he continued to drive the car that had killed Frankie Gotti. On May 28, Favara was forced into a van by three men after he left work. He was never seen again.

The Mohican's daughter

Victoria Gotti—the daughter of John Gotti—wrote a crime novel titled *The Senator's Daughter*, which revolves around the murder of a handsome character who is both a good guy and a ruthless criminal. She denies that the book is about her notorious gangster father—who, she says, is not guilty of the charges that landed him a lifetime jail sentence. In fact, after the verdict against her father was announced, she told reporters, "My father is the last of the Mohicans. They don't make men like him any more. They never will."

Questioned about Favara's disappearance, Gotti said that he and his wife had been in Fort Lauderdale, Florida, when his neighbor was abducted. The police, meanwhile, received a tip saying that Favara had been hacked to death with a chain saw—and entombed in a car that was compacted into a square-foot block of scrap metal. Many people concluded that Gotti was behind the apparent murder. But others—including police detectives—suspected that the kidnapping had been performed without Gotti's blessing—as an attempt to win approval from Gotti and his crew. Favara's body was never found—and no one was ever charged in his kidnapping.

A KISS IS JUST A KISS

In December 1985, FBI agents who kept Gotti under surveillance noticed that he had begun to receive unusual respect from other mobsters. They approached him politely, embraced, and kissed him—a Mafia custom to show respect to a leader. Gotti's status within the mob had changed.

And with good reason. Gotti's mentor, Dellacroce, had died on December 2, 1985. Two weeks later—on December 16, 1985—seventy-two-year-old Gambino boss Paul Castellano was killed in a hail of gunfire outside a Manhattan steak house. And Gotti—who was undoubtedly behind the killing—stepped in to replace the slain mobster as the head of the nation's largest and most powerful Mafia family. No charges were ever brought in Castellano's murder.

THE "TEFLON DON"

By the late 1980s Gotti was on the federal government's wanted list. Brought to trial on charges of racketeering, he faced the possibility of an extended jail term that would inevitably end his reign as one of the youngest dons (bosses) in the history of the Mafia. But on March 13, 1987, Gotti was acquitted of all charges. The U.S. Attorney told the press, "The jury has spoken.

Obviously they perceived there was something wrong with the evidence." But he knew better. The jury had been tampered with. The jury's foreman had been bribed to make sure that Gotti was not convicted. Gotti, who seemed immune (protected) from the law, became known as "the Teflon don" because government prosecutors were unable to make criminal charges against him stick.

That is, until 1992. The Justice Department, which had spent an estimated $75 million to monitor the Mafia don's private conversations, had tapes that provided evidence of Gotti's involvement in mob-related murder and racketeering. A federal judge ruled that Bruce Cutler, Gotti's attorney in the previous trial, could not defend him. Because Cutler was included in some of the recorded conversations used as evidence against

John Gotti, in the doorway, leaves the Ravenite Club in New York City after a party on February 9, 1990, celebrating his being found not guilty of conspiracy and assault. Underboss Salvatore Gravano is seen in front of Gotti.

"Sammy the Bull"

Gotti's top aide, "Sammy the Bull" Gravano, was indicted—along with his boss—for racketeering and murder. Before standing trial, Gravano became an informant against Gotti—in exchange for a guarantee that he would receive no more than a twenty-year sentence. (Without making a deal with the government, Gravano faced a probable sentence of life imprisonment with no possibility of parole.) While he waited to testify, Gravano was held in a safe house (secret location used to keep witnesses safe) in Virginia to ensure that he was not assassinated by Mafia hitmen before the case went to trial.

Gotti, his participation in the trial was considered to be a conflict of interest. The jury was sequestered (put in seclusion) to prevent any tampering. And Salvatore "Sammy the Bull" Gravano—Gotti's right-hand man—was prepared to testify against his former boss.

By the end of the trial, every one of the fourteen counts against Gotti had stuck. James Fox, the assistant director of the FBI in New York, told the press, "The Teflon is gone. The don is covered with Velcro [a material to which almost everything sticks] and every charge stuck." Convicted of racketeering and murder charges, Gotti was sentenced to life imprisonment without the possibility of parole.

Sources for Further Reading

Angelo, Bonnie. "Wanted: A New Godfather." *Time* (April 13, 1992), p. 30.

Blum, Howard. "How the Feds Got Gotti." *New York* (October 25, 1993), pp. 50–59.

Blum, Howard. "How the Feds Got Gotti." *New York* (November 1, 1993), pp. 42–49.

Daly, Michael. "The New Godfather, The Rise of John Gotti." *New York* (June 23, 1986), pp. 28–39.

"John Gotti, Cultivating a Commanding Presence Both Inside and Outside the Courtroom." *The New York Times Biographical Service* (March 1987), p. 216.

Rogers, Patrick. "Don's Delight." *People Weekly* (March 3, 1997), p. 110+.

Sifakis, Carl. *The Mafia Encyclopedia.* New York: Facts on File, 1982, pp. 143–145.

Stone, Michael. "After Gotti." *New York* (February 3, 1992), pp. 22–30.

Virginia Hill

Born: 1918
Died: March 25, 1966

*Referred to by newspapers as "the Queen of the Mob,"
Virginia Hill never actually wielded any authority in the
underworld. Rather, she was infamous for her series of
gangland husbands and lovers—and for acting as a Mafia
go-between and courier.*

POOR AND SHOELESS

Virginia Hill was the sixth of ten children. Her family lived in Liscomb, Alabama—an impoverished steel town where her father worked as a livery stableman. Hill's family was reportedly so poor that, as a child, Virginia never owned or wore a pair of shoes. As an adult, Hill told many stories about her life. She claimed to have been born in the Netherlands and sometimes said that her father was half Native American. She often said she had been married as a teenager. She also claimed that she had become rich by investing an annulment settlement (a payment that results from a marriage that is nullified, or canceled). But no one was ever able to find any record of her supposed first husband, George Rogers.

At age sixteen, Hill ran away from her Alabama home. Settling in Chicago, she worked at the Worlds' Fair—either as a dancer or short-order cook. There she met Joe Epstein, an accountant who was closely involved with the Mafia. A bookie and a gambler, Epstein worked as a tax expert for **Al Capone**'s

The Kefauver Committee

Formed as the Senate Special Committee to Investigate Organized Crime in Interstate Commerce, the Kefauver Committee, as it was known, was named after Senator Estes Kefauver. Looking to make a name for himself in his first term in the Senate, Kefauver sponsored the resolution that created the committee. He also served as the committee's chairman. A Texas Democrat, Kefauver had to overcome stiff opposition from older senators who distrusted their junior colleague's ambitions. The Kefauver Committee has been called "probably the most important probe of organized crime" in the history of the United States. The committee's hearings revealed criminal operations that earned millions of dollars yearly. The hearings also exposed the activities of corrupt public officials who helped the operations to thrive.

During the hearings, many of the crime figures questioned called on their constitutional right against self-incrimination (offering testimony that would prove them guilty of a crime) guaranteed in the Fifth Amendment. In fact, so many criminals cited their constitutional right that "taking the Fifth" became part of the national vocabulary. Others tried to avoid appearing before the committee altogether. "Kefauveritis" was the name given to the variety of mysterious ailments that suddenly afflicted gangsters on the day they were scheduled to testify.

Probably the most dramatic hearings in the Kefauver investigation were those held in New York City. Frank Costello, considered the head of the New York-Miami syndicate (association), testified only on the condition that his face not be shown on television. The cameras focused on his hands for the duration of his appearance. But the ploy failed to protect the gangster's identity. By the time the committee was through with him, Costello was a ruined man. His testimony

(see entry) gang. After he introduced Hill to many prominent members of the Chicago underworld, she quickly became well-known in Mafia circles in Chicago as well as New York and Hollywood.

In the late 1930s, the "new" Mafia was in the process of transforming its activities from small, local operations to large-scale organized crime that linked together criminals throughout the country. A natural actress and diplomat (a skilled negotiator), Hill worked as a go-between and courier for the Mob. On trips between Chicago and New York, she brought news from one Mafia boss to another—so that they were able to communicate

had made him an unwelcome presence among both his legitimate and underworld associates. The other star of the New York hearings was Virginia Hill—whom newspapers called the "Queen of the Mob."

The mobsters who testified at the hearings did not freely provide details about the Mafia's activities. In fact, most of the gangsters who testified denied ever having even *heard* the word Mafia before. But committee members nonetheless managed to piece together a picture of organized crime in America in the 1950s. It was dominated by two syndicates, one operating in New York and the other based in Chicago. Both also had operations in Florida. The committee claimed—but was never completely able to prove—that both of these syndicates were governed by Lucky Luciano.

After the end of the hearings, Kefauver claimed that the committee had done the nation a service. Many of the methods and faces of organized crime had been exposed to the public for the first time. Privately funded crime committees were formed around the country to address criminal activity at the local level. The Justice Department and Internal Revenue Service stepped up efforts to prosecute mobsters on racketeering charges—as well as for failing to pay income taxes. And voters rejected candidates with links to the underworld. Still, for all the public interest generated by the hearings, concrete results were harder to measure. As William Howard Moore wrote in *The Kefauver Committee and the Politics of Crime* (1974), "So inadequate are crime statistics and definitions . . . no one can document whether organized crime and corruption declined or increased during the 1950s."

with one another without fear of being observed by government officials. Hill also worked as a "bag woman." Traveling to Europe with enormous sums of Mafia money, she deposited the funds into Swiss bank accounts and other secret shelters. By having a bag woman hide the money in secret accounts, the Mafia was able to avoid having the sources of its income traced—sources that would reveal the mob's illegal activities.

A MAFIA MAGNET

Hill was linked with a number of powerful Mafiosi (members of the Mafia), including Tony Accardo, Joe Adonis, **Frank**

Costello, (see entry) the Fischetti brothers, Murray Humphreys, Frank Nitti, and **Bugsy Siegel** (see entry). Siegel was said to be her true love. She once commented, "I just seem to be drawn to underworld characters like a magnet."

Handsomely paid for her mob activities, her life was far removed from her impoverished childhood. She lived in lavish houses and threw parties that cost thousands of dollars. She bought extravagant evening gowns and hundreds of pairs of shoes. She traveled to high-priced resorts and tipped so well that bellboys reportedly fought to carry her bags.

A PUBLIC FIGURE

Hill first attracted the public's notice in 1947 when her boyfriend, mobster Bugsy Siegel, was shot to death in a gangland killing in the living room of her house in Beverly Hills, California. Hill was out of the country at the time—which led many people to speculate that the hit was about to take place. The mob suspected that Siegel had been pocketing mob money while he was building the Flamingo Hotel and Casino in Las Vegas, Nevada. Further, they suspected that Siegel used Hill to move the money to Switzerland.

Hill later became a household name when she appeared as a key witness before the Senate Special Committee to Investigate Organized Crime in Interstate Commerce—commonly known as the Kefauver Committee (see box). In a May 1951 appearance that was seen by millions of people who watched the televised coverage, Hill claimed to have a very poor memory, and was therefore unable to explain how she was able to afford her extravagant lifestyle. Much of her testimony was made up. And when she was questioned on her association with Mafia members, Hill shocked the committeemen with an off-color response. Hill also attracted attention for her behavior outside of the hearings. Angered by the press who hounded her, she punched New York reporter Marjorie Farnsworth in the jaw. And she told the others, "I hope an atom bomb falls on all of you!"

THE END OF THE LINE

Hill left the United States later in 1951 to avoid being questioned by the government about back taxes (unpaid tax bills). On June 23, 1954, a federal grand jury formally charged her with income tax evasion for failing to pay more than $160,000 in back taxes. The following year, the Internal Revenue Service (IRS) issued a notice for her arrest. It described her as: "White; female; height 5 feet 4 inches; complexion fair; hair auburn; eyes gray." The notice listed no occupation for Hill, but referred to her as "paramour [lover] and associate of racketeers and gangsters," and gave *twenty-two* aliases, or false names, that she used.

Living in Austria, Hill continued to enjoy a comfortable existence. She experimented with gourmet cooking and looked

Virginia Hill's home in Beverly Hills, where Bugsy Siegel was slain on June 20, 1947.

Bugsy (1991) stars Warren Beatty as the 1940s gangster who built the Flamingo Hotel in Las Vegas, Nevada, when the area was still desert land. Annette Bening plays Bugsy's moll (mistress of a gangster), Virginia Hill, who inspired him to carry out his dream of building the Flamingo (which was her nickname).

Married to the Mob (1988) is the comic story of an attractive Mafia widow (Michelle Pfeiffer) who tries to escape mob life. She ends up fighting off amorous advances from the current mob boss while she is wooed by an undercover cop.

after her teenage son, who was studying to be a waiter. Often recognized by American tourists, she once complained, "All these jerks watch me like I was on exhibition." Hill attempted to commit suicide several times and finally succeeded in March 1966. After she had been missing for two days, her body was found in the snow in the village of Koppl, near Salzburg, Austria. Having taken an overdose of sleeping pills, she died at the age of forty-nine.

Sources for Further Reading

"The Auction Party for Virginia Hill." *American Mercury* (November 1951), pp. 124–128.

Mortimer, Lee. "Virginia Hill's Success Secrets." *American Mercury* (June 1951), pp. 662–669.

Sifakis, Carl. *The Mafia Encyclopedia.* New York: Facts on File, 1982, pp. 152–153.

"Virginia Hill." *The New York Times Obituaries* (March 25, 1966), p. 57.

Meyer Lansky

Born: 1902
Died: January 15, 1983

The newspapers called Meyer Lansky "the Godfather's Godfather" because he was considered to be the genius behind many of the mob's profitable operations. Described as nearly invisible, his role in the Mafia was sometimes downplayed, although some historians believe he was equal—and perhaps superior—to Mafia godfather Lucky Luciano.

BORN ON THE FOURTH OF JULY

Lansky was born in Grodno, Poland, in 1902. When he was nine years old he immigrated to the United States with his parents, Yetta and Max Suchowljansky, and his younger brother and sister. Because his parents could not remember their son's birth date, an immigration officer at Ellis Island, New York, made one up. Lansky was given a July 4 birthday. Born Mair Suchowljansky, he later Americanized his name, calling himself Meyer Lansky.

The Suchowljanskys settled into the Lower East Side of New York City, on the Brooklyn side of the East River. The poor and crime-ridden immigrant neighborhood was dominated by groups of petty criminals, including Kid Dropper's and Little Augie's gangs. Lansky attended Public School 34, where he was a good student whose teachers and fellow classmates saw him as a sharp, self-assured young man. Lansky graduated from the eighth grade in 1917 and soon went to work in a tool and die shop on the Lower East Side. Already involved in shady (criminal)

Israeli author Uri Dan claims that Lansky felt an intense connection to other Jews. In *Meyer Lansky, Mogul of the Mob,* he explains:

In [Lansky's] eyes we Israelis had been molded by blood, violence, and a struggle for survival and power in the sands of the Middle East. Meyer perceived his background on New York's Lower East Side as similar, though in a different setting. He felt a kinship with me that transcended generations, cultures, and continents.

activities, he added to his income by organizing a floating dice game. (A floating dice game is held at different locations in order to prevent law enforcers from breaking it up).

THE BUGS-MEYER GANG

Lansky was first arrested at the age of sixteen. On October 24, 1918, he rushed into an abandoned tenement (housing unit), where someone was screaming. He found a young man attacking a woman and boy. The police arrived just in time to see him strike the young man. Charged with assault, Lansky was let go after he paid a $2 fine. But the incident did not end there. The young man he had struck—Lucky Luciano—and the boy he had saved—**Bugsy Siegel** (see entry)— would both become important criminal associates in Lansky's adult life.

During the 1920s, as Prohibition (when the Eighteenth Amendment outlawed the manufacture and sale of alcohol) went into effect, Lansky and Siegel worked side-by-side in the bootlegging business. Working as shotgun riders, they protected illegal shipments of alcohol as they were transported by various gangs operating in New York and New Jersey. Lansky and Siegel also hijacked the liquor shipments of other gangsters—a practice that required violent methods. By 1928 the two had formed a gang of their own—called the Bugs-Meyer Mob. In addition to transporting illegal liquor—an activity known as rumrunning—the gang sold its services to bootleggers and other criminals. Some described the Bugs-Meyer Mob as the most violent Prohibition-era gang in the East. Lansky and Siegel eventually joined a group of East Coast gangs that banded together to coordinate rumrunning in the area. Lansky was made the controller (financial supervisor) of the group, which was called the Eastern syndicate.

THE LAUNDRY BUSINESS

When Prohibition ended in December 1933, Lansky and Siegel were wealthy men. Lansky invested his profits in both legal and illegal enterprises, and soon became involved in crooked gambling casinos in Florida, New Orleans, and upstate New York. By 1934 he had become an important figure in the mob's efforts to re-invent itself as a nationwide crime syndicate. A loose assembly of various gangs, the syndicate was governed by a board of top mobsters who coordinated the activities of gangs across the country. The syndicate's first top man—called the "first among equals"—was Lucky Luciano. A longtime associate of Lansky's, Luciano respected his sharp intellect and shrewd (cunning) ability to look ahead. Under Luciano's supervision, Lansky devised numerous schemes to transform the syndicate into a bigger, more diversified—and more profitable— enterprise.

Chairman of the board

According to an FBI agent who was familiar with the mobster's brilliant plans and financial scams, "[Lansky] would have been chairman of the board of General Motors if he'd gone into legitimate [legal] business." But Lansky devoted his efforts to underworld activities. Some people referred to him as the "Chairman of the Board of the National Crime Syndicate."

Lansky moved immediately into organized gambling. A mathematics genius, he provided the basic groundwork of modern resort gambling—a wildly profitable source of income. Mobsters reaped huge profits by "skimming" funds from the counting rooms of the casinos. But the syndicate needed to cover its tracks. The skimmed money was worthless until its illegal origins could be hidden.

Lansky came up with ingenious methods for "laundering" money (taking money illegally obtained and using it for legitimate purposes)—which was then hidden or invested. He developed a network of bankers, couriers, go-betweens, and frontmen that extended throughout the world. He arranged to route the profits of gambling and other illegal activities to foreign banks, through layers of dummy (fake) corporations.

By the time the money returned to the United States, its origins were untraceable. Sometimes it was invested in legitimate (legal) businesses. Often it was "lent" to gangsters, who were, in essence, lending money to themselves. Middlemen sometimes lent syndicate money to legitimate businessmen—who repaid the loans plus a steep interest rate (an additional fee that increased over time). Lansky's schemes were the work of a financial whiz. The syndicate was free to enjoy hundreds of thousands of dollars that could not be traced to the organization's illegal activities.

November 17, 1952.
Meyer Lansky (second
from right) confers
with (from left to
right) attorneys Edward
Sullivan, Thomas
Clancy, and Moses
Polakoff. Lansky was
about to go on trial on
charges of conspiracy,
gambling, and forgery.

A Cuban gold mine

Lansky also masterminded what was for a while the syndicate's most profitable endeavor—gambling in Havana, Cuba.
He convinced Cuban dictator Fulgencio Batista to guarantee
him a monopoly (exclusive control) of gambling in the country.
He also managed to have a law passed that permitted gambling
only in hotels that were worth at least $1 million. He then over-
saw the construction of the only million-dollar establishments
in Havana—and placed syndicate friends in control of the gambling operations. Lansky reportedly deposited $3 million in a
Swiss bank for Batista—in addition to paying the military
leader 50 percent of the casino profits. Havana was for a while a
gambling paradise. But when Batista was over-thrown by Fidel
Castro (who became the Cuban premier in 1959), Lansky's

dream went up in smoke. Castro's revolution-
aries wanted no part of the syndicate's
money-making schemes.

THE TAX MAN

In 1970 the federal government set out to
convict Lansky. Many gangsters, like Lansky,
enjoyed money that had been skimmed from
casinos in Las Vegas that were secretly owned
by the syndicate. And many were convicted
for income tax evasion. But Lansky was not
an easy target. He did not flaunt (show off)
his wealth: he led a quiet, modest life.

Clean money

Lansky arranged for middlemen to
deposit hundreds of thousands of dollars in
mob profits in secret accounts in Switzerland.
Because Swiss banks do not reveal the name
of depositors, there is no way to find out to
whom the money belongs. Money laundered
through Swiss bank accounts was said to have
been washed clean in the snow of the Alps.

Rather than face two federal indictments, Lansky left the
country. (The U.S. government was also attempting to have
Lansky deported as an undesirable alien). Traveling to Israel, he
hoped to remain in the country under the Law of the Return—
which gives anyone who was born to a Jewish mother the right
to claim Israeli citizenship. Lansky reportedly invested millions
of dollars in the country while his application for citizenship
was being considered. But Israeli officials were concerned that
the mobster might move his criminal activities to his adoptive
country. U.S. officials were strongly opposed to his bid for
Israeli citizenship. Some historians claim that the administra-
tion of President Richard M. Nixon threatened to hold back
Phantom jets that had been promised to Israel if Lansky were
allowed to stay. After much public debate, Lansky was forced
out of the country in 1972.

The following year Lansky went to trial in Miami, Florida.
Charged with income tax evasion, he was acquitted (found not
guilty). Following the trial, the government abandoned its cru-
sade to convict the man who was sometimes called the "Godfather's Godfather." Lansky lived peacefully with his wife in a
high-security condominium for almost another decade. He died
of cancer in a New York hospital on January 15, 1983. He was
eighty-one years old.

Sources for Further Reading

Fried, Alfred. *The Rise and Fall of the Jewish Gangster in America.*
  Austin, TX: Holt, Rinehart and Winston, 1988, pp. 229–286.

Take a look at this!

The Godfather, Part II (1974) continues the story of the Corleone family. Hyman Roth, a character played by Lee Strasberg in the film, was modeled after Meyer Lansky. Soon after the movie was released in 1974, the actor received a phone call from a man who did not identify himself. "You did good," the man said. "Now why couldn't you have made me more sympathetic?"

Gage, Nicholas. "The Little Big Man Who Laughs at the Law." *Atlantic Monthly* (July 1970), pp. 62–69.

"Meyer Lansky." *The New York Times Obituaries* (January 16, 1983), p. 29.

"Meyer Lansky: Mogul of the Mob." *The New Republic* (January 19, 1980), pp. 36–38.

Sheppard, R. Z. "Low Profile, Little Man: Meyer Lansky and the Gangster Life." *Time* (November 4, 1991), p. 93.

Sifakis, Carl. *The Mafia Encyclopedia.* New York: Facts on File, 1982.

The
Purple Gang
Active: c. 1918-c. 1932

*Made up of the children of poor Jewish immigrants, the Purple Gang started out as a
small band of street thugs. But with the prohibition of the sale of liquor in Michigan,
the gang rose to the top of the Detroit underworld.*

LITTLE JERUSALEM

The Purple Gang was considered to be one of the most ruthless and violent gangs of the Prohibition era (when the Eighteenth Amendment outlawed the manufacture and sale of
liquor from 1919 to 1933). Most of the original members came
from the lower east side of Detroit, Michigan. The area—a ghetto referred to as "Little Jerusalem" because of the number of
Jewish immigrants who lived there—was impoverished, crime-
ridden, and plagued by violence. Prior to 1918, the gang consisted entirely of Jewish youths. Most were the children of hard-
working Russian Jews who had recently immigrated to the
United States. The gang was led by four brothers, Abe, Isadore
(Izzy), Joe, and Raymond Bernstein, along with Harry and
Louis Fleischer.

A BOOTLEG EMPIRE

Prohibition was enacted in Michigan in May 1918. The
city—separated from Canada by the Detroit River—was an

Harry Fleisher.

important center for bootleggers who smuggled booze across the border from Canada, where the production of alcohol was not outlawed. The Purple Gang quickly established itself as a powerful criminal force in Detroit. Formerly a loosely organized group of street hoodlums, the Purples had the seeds of an organized criminal network when Prohibition hit Detroit. The gang soon moved into extortion (obtaining money through force or intimidation), armed robbery, hijacking, gambling, jewel robbery, prostitution, loan-sharking, and bootlegging.

The Purple Gang first entered the liquor racket by offering "protection" to bootleggers. Bootleggers were often preyed on by other gangsters who hijacked their cargoes. The Purples collected a fee—or a share in the profits—for protecting more established gangsters as they unloaded shipments of alcohol on the Detroit waterfront. Gangsters who refused to pay for protection were often robbed of their shipments by the very gang that had promised them protection. The Purples earned a reputation as ruthless killers who readily murdered other gangsters in order to hijack their illegal loads. The gang eventually became involved in transporting liquor to Chicago and other large Midwestern cities. **Al Capone** (see entry), who ruled the Chicago underworld, relied on the Purple Gang to deliver Canadian whiskey to his organization. Aware of the Purple Gang's savage reputation, Capone allowed them to operate as his agents—rather than risk a bloody battle in an attempt to take over their operations.

By the late 1920s, the Purple Gang had expanded to include recruits from Chicago, New York, and St. Louis. No longer an exclusively Jewish organization, the gang had many Italian members, such as Frank and Vincent Camerata, James and Peter Licavoli, Joseph Massei, and Joseph Zerilli—all of whom later became prominent criminal figures.

The Milaflores Massacre and the Cleaners' War

In March 1926, Purple Gang members were responsible for a machine-gun ambush in the Milaflores Apartments at 106 Alexandrine Avenue East in an apartment belonging to Abe Axler and Edward Fletcher. The three men who died in the ambush—Frank Wright, Reuben Cohen, and Joseph Bloom—were suspected of killing a Purple Gang liquor distributor. Although the Purple Gang was blamed for the slayings, the police were never able to locate the killers, who included Fred "Killer" Burke (later a participant in the St. Valentine's Day Massacre in Chicago) and two other gunmen.

The Purples profited from a period of unrest in the cleaning industry in Detroit. Working as hired muscle for dishonest labor leaders, they bullied union members. They also threatened non-union (independent) workers in what became known as the Cleaners and Dyers War. Paid well to enforce the union's policy, they relied on violent methods—such as beatings, bombings, kidnappings, theft, and murder—to keep the workers in line. In 1928, the Purple Gang trial ended the union dispute. But all of the Purple defendants were eventually found not guilty of extortion and released, and the gang continued to thrive as Detroit's foremost criminal organization.

Eddie Fletcher.

The Collingwood Manor Massacre

By the 1930s, members of the Purple Gang had begun to fight among themselves. Three Purples—Joe Lebowitz, Hymie Paul, and Isadore "Joe" Sutker—formed what was called the "Little Jewish Navy." Using several boats, they transported liquor from Canada—a practice known as "rumrunning." They also practiced hijacking, and had begun to expand their operations beyond the area that was assigned to them by the leaders of the Purple Gang. Lebowitz, Paul, and Sutker planned eventu-

Bloody valentine

The Purples had a reputation as a bloody, violent gang. Al Capone reportedly called on three of the Purple Gang's hitmen--George Lewis and Phil and Harry Keywell--to help pull off the St. Valentine's Day Massacre in 1929.

Detroit, Michigan, as seen across the Detroit River from Windsor, Ontario, Canada, in the early 1900s.

ally to form their own organization—something that seriously displeased the leadership of the Purples.

On September 16, 1931, the three men attended what they believed to be a peaceful meeting at an apartment on Collingwood Avenue. They were escorted by a bookie named Sol Levine. When they arrived at the apartment, a brief discussion followed—after which the three unarmed men were shot to death by Purple gangsters. Arrested by the police shortly thereafter, Levine became a state's witness in the affair. Based on his testimony, three Purple gangsters were arrested and tried for first-degree murder. Raymond Bernstein, Harry Keywell, and Irving Milberg were convicted and sentenced to life in prison for their role in what became known as the Collingwood Manor massacre.

Eventually, the Purples were invited to join the national crime syndicate that had been formed in the 1930s under the leadership of Lucky Luciano and **Meyer Lansky** (see entry). The gang was absorbed into the larger syndicate, and became an important aspect of the mob's gambling activities.

Sources for Further Reading

Carpozi, Balsamo and George Carpozi. *Under the Clock, The Inside Story of the Mafia's First Hundred Years.* Far Hills, NJ: New Horizon Press, 1988, pp. 36–39.

Fried, Albert. *The Rise and Fall of the Jewish Gangster in America.* Holt, Rinehart and Winston, 1988, pp. 103–122.

A History of Detroit Organized Crime. [Online] Available http://detnews.com/1998/metro/9801/25/01250053.html, November 19, 1997.

Nash, Jay Robert. *Bloodletters and Badmen.* New York: M. Evans, 1973, pp. 454–455.

Sifakis, Carl. *The Mafia Encyclopedia.* New York: Facts on File, 1982, pp. 268–269.

A colorful name

There are a number of theories about how the Purple Gang received its name. Some say the Purples were named after an early leader, Samuel "Sammy Purple" Cohen. Others cite the gangsters' workout wardrobe. Gang member Eddie Fletcher regularly wore a purple jersey when he worked out at a local gym, and the gang's other members soon followed his example. Probably the most popular theory is that the name was coined by street merchants in Detroit's Hasting Street quarter. The shopkeepers referred to the gangsters as Purples because they were "tainted," or "off-color"—like the color of spoiled meat.

Bugsy Siegel
(Benjamin Siegel)

Born: February 28, 1906
Died: June 20, 1947

As a gangster who ran gambling rackets, Bugsy Siegel was something of a forward-thinker. As part of an expansion of gambling activities in the West, he is credited with putting the small Nevada town of Las Vegas on the map as the kingdom of world gambling capitals.

A HELLION IN HELL'S KITCHEN

Benjamin "Bugsy" Siegel was born on February 28, 1906, in Brooklyn, New York. His poor Jewish parents lived in a crime-ridden slum known as Hell's Kitchen—the breeding ground for many criminals of that era. Among Siegel's boyhood friends were George Raft, who later established a movie career playing gangster roles, and Bo Weinberg, later a top aide to gangster **Dutch Schultz** (see entry).

In a manner similar to fellow gangster **Louis Lepke** (see entry), Siegel began his criminal career by preying upon push-cart peddlers on the Lower East Side with a sidekick named Morris "Moey" Sedway. Unlike Lepke, Siegel did not usually beat the vendors he was trying to convince to buy protection from him. Rather he would simply have Sedway pour kerosene (a fuel oil) over the vendors' merchandise and then light it on fire. It usually only took a vendor one lesson to decide to pay the "insurance."

By the time he was fourteen years old, Siegel was in charge of his own gang of criminals. He joined forces with **Meyer Lan-**

sky (see entry), another rising young New York gangster, to create the Bugs-Meyer Mob. Members of the mob hired their services as enforcers for the large bootlegging mobs. Less than ten years later, the enforcement arm of the mob known as "Murder, Inc." took over responsibility for gangland killings. The Bugs-Meyer Mob was involved in a number of other activities as well. The young mobsters ambushed rival gangsters and took their liquor shipments. They also dealt in stolen cars, prostitution, drug trafficking, and gambling rackets in New York, New Jersey, and Pennsylvania.

AN INTERESTING VACATION

During a trip to Italy with Countess Dorothy Dendice Taylor DiFrasso—one of the gangster's many girlfriends—Siegel met German Nazi leaders Hermann Goering and Joseph Goebbels. He despised both men—for personal reasons. According to rumor, Siegel would have killed the two Germans—who later became involved in Nazi crimes during World War II—if DiFrasso had not stopped him.

A SEASONED HIT MAN

Throughout the 1920s and 1930s, Siegel continued to climb up the underworld ladder. At the same time, Luciano and a number of other Italian gangsters began to organize criminal mobs into a national organization, or syndicate. Siegel and Lansky—who were both Jewish—were included in the organization. The mob's reorganization required some "housecleaning"—the killing of veteran gangsters who stood in the way of the syndicate's progress. Siegel was an eager participant in the new mob's clean-up jobs. In 1931, he was one of the hit men who assassinated Joe "the Boss" Maseria— an old-guard gangster—at a restaurant in Coney Island, New York. Siegel was often accompanied by killer Frankie Carbo, who later became the head of the mob's prizefighting (boxing) racket.

Not all of Siegel's killings were ordered by the national syndicate. In 1935, the government charged syndicate member Dutch Schultz with income tax evasion. Certain Schultz's career would be cut short by imprisonment, fellow syndicate members Luciano and Vito Genovese took over "the Dutchman's" profitable numbers rackets in Harlem. They did this with the help of Schultz's top lieutenant, Bo Weinberg. Tried in upper New York State, Schultz managed to avoid conviction. When he returned to New York City, he found his empire sacked. Aware that his former aide had turned traitor, he ordered Weinberg's assassination. Siegel— who had grown up with Weinberg—was the hit man.

The top man at Murder, Inc.

Louis Lepke (see entry) had the questionable distinction of being executed as the indirect result of founding and building a very successful, though illegal, business. A famous gangster of the 1930s and 1940s, he is perhaps best known by the name of his business, Murder, Inc.

Criminal Education

Lepke, as he was popularly known, was born Louis Buchalter in Manhattan, New York. His only known occupation was as a criminal. He graduated from simple pushcart robberies at the age of seventeen. Lepke was short—five feet seven and one-half inches tall. To threaten those he sought to "protect," he joined forces with Jacob Gurrah Shapiro, a huge man he had met when both gangsters tried to rob the same pushcart. They joined the Lower East Side gang and worked in establishing control over the city's garment industry.

On October 15, 1926, Lepke machine-gunned Jacob "Little Augie" Orgen to death and assumed the position of undisputed leader of the city's garment and business rackets. Often described as the "brains of the operation," Lepke began recruiting mainly Jewish criminals from other gangs to establish his own hit teams.

He also continued to intimidate unions. At one point, his organization controlled the four-hundred-thousand member Clothing Workers Union as well as trucking and motion-picture operators unions. By 1932, Lepke had helped establish a national crime syndicate with other notable gangsters such as Bugsy Siegel, Meyer Lansky, Lucky Luciano, **Frank Costello** (see entry), and Albert Anastasia. In 1933, he proposed the establishment of a national enforcement division of the syndicate, made up of hired killers who would go anywhere to assassinate

"Bugsy"

Few people called Benjamin Siegel "Bugsy" to his face. The gangster hated the nickname--which he had acquired for his sometimes crazy behavior and cold-blooded willingness to kill.

CALIFORNIA DREAMING

Eventually, Siegel became the target of numerous attempts against his life. With the heat turned up, he reportedly approached syndicate leaders regarding a plan to combine criminal undertakings in California with Jack Dragna, who at the time controlled the underworld in that state. With Dragna's help, Siegel operated various gambling establishments, including a floating casino.

The gangsters' other activities included drug smuggling. Using a series of relay points, they were able to transport narcotics from Mexico into the United States without being detected by legal authorities. They also employed a relay system to establish a bookmaking wire service. The wire service transmit-

those who opposed the syndicate. Murder, Inc. was born.

The Fix is In

By the end of the 1930s, Lepke's crime operation was so large that he was having trouble controlling all of it. Murder, Inc., employed so many hired killers that it was only a matter of time before some of them began to crack and provide information to the authorities when they were caught for murdering someone. One of the killers, Max Rubin, eventually implicated Lepke in the killing of Joseph Rosen.

In 1939, Moey Wolinsky had advised Lepke that the syndicate board had decided that he should turn himself in to be tried on narcotics charges, taking the police pressure off the mob. Wolinsky also told him that, as part of the deal, the "fix was in" and Lepke would not be turned over to the New York authorities to be tried for Rosen's murder.

Execution

While Lepke was serving a fourteen-year sentence on narcotics charges, he was tried and found guilty of the murder of Rosen. He was sentenced to die in the electric chair. As it turned out, there was no deal to prevent Lepke from being turned over to the New York authorities. He had been double-crossed.

Lepke fought the guilty verdict sentence for years. During that time he continued to issue orders through Murder, Inc., to kill those who had betrayed him—including Abe "Kid Twist" Reles, one of the first to implicate him for murder. Reles later fell from a hotel window while under police protection. Lepke also ordered the murder of Wolinsky, who was shot to death in 1943. Lepke was electrocuted in Sing Sing prison in New York on March 4, 1944. He was the only highly placed member of the national crime syndicate ever to be legally executed.

ted the results of West Coast horse races to bookies who collected bets in the East and elsewhere.

In California, Siegel contacted his boyhood friend, actor George Raft, who reportedly liked the gangster and was happy to introduce him to various actors and studio directors. A well-dressed, handsome man, Siegel had a boyish, charming personality. He rubbed elbows with many Hollywood stars, including Clark Gable, Jean Harlow, Cary Grant, and Gary Cooper.

A DESERT OASIS

By the mid-1940s, Lansky had gained a reputation as the "chairman of the board" of the national crime syndicate. In

1945, Lansky and Siegel decided to establish a gambling hotel in a small town called Las Vegas, Nevada. According to reports, Siegel borrowed $3 million from the syndicate and eventually spent $6 million in building the Flamingo Hotel. (Flamingo was the nickname of one of Siegel's girlfriends, **Virginia Hill** [see entry].) As the first legalized gambling casino in the United States, the Flamingo became famous nationwide, and Siegel drew enormous profits from it.

But the syndicate members suspected—with good cause—that Siegel was pocketing money that was not his. They believed that the money—which came from building funds and gambling income—had been stashed in Swiss bank accounts by Siegel's mistress, Hill.

A BAD ROLL OF THE DICE

On behalf of the syndicate, Luciano contacted Siegel and instructed him to meet with syndicate members in Havana, Cuba. Havana was at that time one of the gambling centers of the world and a gangster haven. At the Havana meeting in December 1946, Siegel denied that he had stolen mob money. Apparently syndicate members did not believe him.

On June 20, 1947, as Siegel sat in the living room of Hill's Beverly Hills mansion, he was gunned down by shotgun fire. (Hill was in Europe at the time.) Struck three times, he died instantly. When law enforcement officials arrived at the scene of the slaying, they found the gangster's right eye in the dining room, five yards from the corpse. The forty-one-year-old mobster was buried in a closed casket.

Although Lansky and Luciano denied involvement in the hit, there is little doubt that Siegel was murdered on syndicate orders. Carbo is commonly believed to have been the gunman who fired into the living room of Hill's mansion on Linden Drive. Shortly after Siegel's assassination, Sedway and several syndicate members appeared at the Flamingo Hotel and informed the manager that they were taking over.

Sources for Further Reading

Nash, Jay Robert. *Bloodletters and Badmen.* New York: M. Evans, 1973, pp. 501–504.

Sifakis, Carl. *The Mafia Encyclopedia.* New York: Facts on File, 1982, pp. 302–304.

Racketeers
and Gamblers

Underworld figures have for a long time engaged in racketeering, a form of extortion. Today, mobsters practice racketeering to collect substantial kickbacks—and to control certain industries and unions. A steady source of vast power and income, racketeering is a mainstay of modern-day mobsters.

In the mid-1940s, Las Vegas, Nevada, was nothing more than a remote desert town. Through a scheme masterminded by mobster Meyer Lansky—and in part implemented by Bugsy Siegel—the area soon became a gambler's mecca. Today, gambling operations—which produce immense quantities of easily-skimmed cash—constitute a substantial portion of the Mob's activities and income.

In this section you'll meet some of the nation's early racketeers and gamblers. Among those included are Louis Lepke, who murdered his way to the top of New York's labor racketeering empire, and later played a critical role in the formation of a national crime syndicate; Arnold Rothstein, a brilliant organizer—considered by many to be the father of organized crime in America—who was himself a compulsive gambler; and Diamond Joe Esposito, an early practitioner of labor racketeering and political fixing. You'll also read about the formation of Murder, Inc.— a hit squad assembled to carry out the mob's violent dirty work.

65

Frank Costello

Born: January 26, 1891
Died: February 18, 1973
AKA: Frank Saverio, Francisco
Seriglia, Frank Stello

Frank Costello rose from a poor immigrant background to play a critical role in the formation of the national crime syndicate (association). A close associate of the mob's top bosses, he mediated disagreements and earned a reputation as a "fixer" who could take care of any legal difficulties.

A YOUTHFUL OFFENDER

Born Francesco Castiglia in Lauropoli, Calabria, in southwest Italy, Costello was the sixth child of a poor farmer. When he was four he moved with his family to New York's East Harlem, an Italian slum plagued by street crime. His father opened a small grocery on East 108th Street. Costello quit school at the age of eleven to sell newspapers and run a crap game for kids. (Craps is a game in which the participants place bets on the throw of dice.) Running the game required the young Costello to pay-off a neighborhood policeman—a practice that he would use throughout his criminal career.

A petty (small-time) thief by his teens, Costello was arrested for assault and robbery on April 25, 1908. The case was dismissed. When he was twenty-one he was arrested again—for robbing a woman of $1,600 on the street—the charges were also dropped. In 1914, Costello followed his brother, Edward—who was ten years older—into a ruthless Manhattan street gang

Natural born criminal

When Costello became a U.S. citizen in 1925, he listed his occupation as real estate operator. He was, in fact, a bootlegger at the time. Decades later, when government officials found it difficult to convict the mobster of other crimes, they tried to have his citizenship taken away on the grounds that he had lied about his occupation. This, in turn, would have led to his deportation (forcible return) to Italy as an undesirable alien. But Italian authorities protested. Costello, they said, was a product of American society: when he left Italy as a four-year-old, he had no criminal record.

called the "Gophers," run by gangster **Owney Madden** (see entry). As a member of this gang, Costello began to carry a gun.

Arrested a third time, in 1915, Costello was charged with illegal possession of a pistol. At trial he encountered Edward Swann, a strict judge who intended to teach the young hoodlum (criminal) a lesson. According to court records, the judge said:

> I have got it right from his [Costello's] neighbors that he has the reputation of being a gunman and in this particular case he . . . had a very beautiful weapon and was . . . prepared to do the work of a gunman. He was charged on two other occasions with doing the work of a gunman and, somehow or other, got out of it. Now I commit him to the penitentiary for one year. . . .

Costello served ten months in prison on Welfare Island. In spite of accusations of criminal acts and numerous arrests, it would be another thirty-seven years before he returned to prison.

Kewpie dolls and rumrunning

Costello's criminal career blossomed after his release from Welfare Island. Using money and favors to gain political protection, he ran Harlem crap games. He used fruit stores as fronts to hide illegal gambling activities that took place in the back rooms. He became rich from his numerous gambling enterprises, and shared his wealth with policemen and politicians to ensure that his activities would not be hindered by the law. In 1917, after he was drafted into the U.S. Army, Costello used his political contacts to avoid service.

In 1919, Costello became a partner in something called the Horowitz Novelty Company, which produced Kewpie dolls as prizes for punchboard players. Players paid as much as twenty-five cents per punchboard to punch holes in a card to find out whether they had winning numbers. Although the Horowitz

Novelty Company went bankrupt (reduced to financial ruin), it reappeared as the Dainties Products Company, which quickly earned Costello a small fortune.

By 1920, Costello had enough money to invest into the area's booming bootlegging business (illegal manufacture and sale of alcohol). At first he purchased liquor through his various contacts in the city. With his brother's help, he used the threat of violence to force bar owners to purchase his booze. Costello eventually carved out a role as a wholesale supplier to larger, more established gangs. He ran his bootlegging operations like a big business. He traveled to Montreal, Quebec, Canada, to purchase a fortune in high quality whiskey from Canadian and European exporters. He was responsible for the scheduling of speed boats and trucks that carried liquor shipments into New York City under the noses of Prohibition officers. He oversaw staffs of salespeople and bookkeepers who tallied the day-to-day operations. And he supervised the bribery (paid-off) of thousands of policemen who were paid to look the other way.

A FORTUNE IN NICKELS AND DIMES

Aware that Prohibition (when the Eighteenth Amendment outlawed the manufacture and sale of alcohol) was doomed to fail, Costello expanded his operations. During the early 1920s, he controlled the city's developing slot machine business. Between 1928 and 1934, his slot machine business operated as many as five thousand machines—whose profits were estimated at about $600 per machine each year. With a profit of $3 million each year, Costello made a fortune on the nickel-operated machines.

NEW ORLEANS

Costello—whose influence was far-reaching—wasn't about to abandon such a profitable business. At the invitation of Demo-

A day in the life . . .

Costello's routine, as the don (Mafia leader) of the New York underworld, was highly predictable. He once remarked, "I go places so regular they call me Mr. Schedule." A typical day went as follows:

10 a.m.
Shave, manicure—and sometimes a haircut at the barbershop in the Waldorf-Astoria Hotel.

Late morning
Business conversations in the Waldorf lobby.

Lunch
Usually at the Norse Grill in the Waldorf. (Costello was a good tipper.)

Late afternoon
A movie at a theater on Broadway (in Manhattan) or in the suburbs

Evening
Cocktails at the Madison Hotel (never more than three). More business conversations.

In the bag

Manhattan district attorney Frank Hogan obtained permission to place a wiretap (listening device) on Costello's phone in 1943. The mobster's conversations revealed much about his role in New York politics—including his part in helping Thomas Aurelio to the Democratic nomination for state supreme court judge. Hogan taped an August 23 conversation between Costello and Aurelio that revealed the political fix:

Aurelio: "How are you, and thanks for everything."

Costello: "Congratulations. It went over perfect. When I tell you something is in the bag, you can rest assured."

Aurelio: "It was perfect. It was fine."

Costello: "Well, we will all have to get together and have dinner some night real soon."

Aurelio: "That would be fine. But right now I want to assure you of my loyalty for all you have done. It is unwavering."

After the conversation was made public, authorities attempted to have Aurelio disbarred (expelled from the bar, a professional organization of lawyers). They failed. Costello was never punished for his role in the fix, either. The evidence against him relied on the wiretap, which was inadmissible as evidence in court.

cratic Louisiana senator Huey E. Long—who promised to legalize the slot machine trade—Costello set up shop in New Orleans within months of being forced out of New York. Having made a relatively small cash investment, Costello remained in New York while he raked in the profits of his Louisiana enterprise.

Costello's vast profits nearly landed him in jail. In 1939, the federal government tried him in New Orleans on charges of evading (avoiding) taxes on thousands of dollars in hidden income. The government's case was based on the discovery that Costello's declared income could not possibly support his expensive lifestyle. But Costello remained free to purchase expensive pajamas and hand-tailored suits. The government lost its case because of lack of evidence.

ON TOP OF THE WORLD

By the end of the 1920s, Costello had become a top adviser to Lucky Luciano, one of the most powerful crime bosses in the country. Together with **Meyer Lansky** (see entry), Costello and Luciano helped to create a national crime syndicate during the 1930s. Lansky and Luciano organized the activities of criminal gangs that had previously acted independently. Costello continued to do what he did best—ensuring friendly relations with policemen and politicians. He made sure that complaints disappeared, cases were dropped, and sentences shortened. As a skilled negotiator who dealt with policemen, politicians, and judges, he became known as the "Prime Minister" (official head) of the underworld.

By the 1950s, Costello had become one of the most powerful crime figures in the United States. He was an important member of the national syndicate's crime board, which made decisions that governed the actions of gangsters across the country. He is believed to have been responsible for shielding the crime syndicate from the Federal Bureau of Investigation, whose leader, J. Edgar Hoover, denied the existence of organized crime in America.

My fair lady

Even behind bars, Costello was an influential man. One day in late 1957, his lawyer, Edward Bennett Williams, visited him in the Federal House of Detention in New York. Williams made an off-hand remark that he had been unable—at any price—to purchase tickets to "My Fair Lady." Williams wanted to attend the popular theater play to celebrate his thirty-fifth wedding anniversary with his wife and her parents.

Williams left the detention center and shortly after he arrived home, his doorbell rang. A husky man handed him an envelope and left. When he looked inside, he found four tickets to that evening's performance of the play.

That is, until the mayor of New York, Fiorello La Guardia, a fellow Italian, took office. La Guardia objected to the gambling machines—some of which were equipped with ladders so that little children could reach the coin slot to play. Formerly protected by an injunction against police seizure, the machines were seized at the mayor's bequest. (An injunction is a court order forbidding a certain act.) Swinging a sledge hammer, La Guardia personally demolished dozens of machines. The rest he had destroyed and thrown into the sea. By 1935, La Guardia had driven the slot machine business out of New York. And he dismissed crime boss Costello as a bum and a punk.

CONTEMPT

In 1951, a Senate Crime Investigating Committee headed by Senator Estes Kefauver met to investigate organized crime in America. Questioned for eight days in February and March of

that year, Costello testified about his role in New York City politics. The committee ultimately labeled Costello "the number-one racketeer in the country." Among other things, it revealed that the gangster had played an important role in the Democratic nomination of Thomas Aurelio for the New York Supreme Court some eight years earlier.

Costello insisted that his face not be shown on the televised hearings. But the camera recorded his nervous hand movements and raspy voice. Having carefully avoided the limelight throughout his criminal career, Costello found himself thrust into the public eye. On March 15, Costello left the courtroom claiming that he had a sore throat. His refusal to testify further earned him a conviction for contempt (disobeying a legal order) of the committee, for which he was sentenced to eighteen months in prison with a $5,000 fine.

UNCLE FRANK

When he was released from prison, Costello discovered that the unwanted publicity and time behind bars had weakened his position as head of the Luciano crime family. (Costello had assumed leadership after Lucky Luciano was deported for operating a prostitution ring.) Vito Genovese, a rival crime boss, was eager to take over Costello's territory. For a while, Costello managed to stall Genovese, who arranged for the assassination of Costello's aide, Willie Moretti, and his ally (a helpful associate), Albert Anastasia.

On May 2, 1957, Genovese sent Vincent "the Chin" Gigante to ambush his rival. As Costello entered his Central Park West apartment building, Gigante shouted, "This is for you Frank!" and fired several shots. Only slightly wounded by a bullet that grazed his head, Costello survived. But he understood Genovese's message—whether the shooting was intended to be fatal, or, as some claimed, merely a warning. Costello soon began to step back from his gambling operations, and by the early 1960s had officially retired from crime.

Costello and his wife, Loretta "Bobbie" Geigerman Costello, lived quietly, spending time in their Manhattan apartment and Long Island summer home. Fond of being called "Uncle Frank," the former gangster tended a small peach orchard on his summer property, and displayed flowers he had grown in local shows. Despite occasional newspaper stories that claimed he had resumed his position as don of the New York underworld, Costello insisted that he was a law-abiding retiree. When he was legally summoned by a subpoena (pronounced suh-PEE-na) to testify before a grand jury that was investigating gambling, in May, 1970, he told reporters, "I'm retired. I don't know any more about this than you do." Costello died of natural causes on February 18, 1973, at the age of eighty-two.

An honest New Yorker

After he retired, Costello had a hard time convincing the public that was nothing more than a law-abiding citizen. He once told reporters, "Right now I'm cleaner than 99 percent of New Yorkers. Now I don't want you to get the wrong impression—I never sold any Bibles."

Sources for Further Reading

"Costello, Frank." *The New York Times Obituaries* (February 19, 1973), pp. 1, 21.

"Manners & Morals." *Time* (November 28, 1949), pp. 15–18.

"The Men Behind the Tiger." *The Nation* (October 31, 1959), pp. 265–269.

Sifakis, Carl. *The Mafia Encyclopedia.* New York: Facts on File, 1982, pp. 185–188.

Who's Who in the Mafia. [Online] Available http://home1.pacific.net.sg/~seowjean/Mafia/mafia.html, November 7, 1997.

Legs Diamond
(John Thomas Diamond)

Born: 1896
Died: December 17, 1931

A former member of a vicious youth gang, Legs Diamond muscled his way to the top of the bootlegging business in Prohibition-era New York. At one time rumored to be impossible to kill, he died in a gangland execution.

THE SON OF IRISH IMMIGRANTS

John Thomas Diamond was born in 1896, in Kensington, a poor enclave (area) of Irish immigrants in Philadelphia, Pennsylvania. His parents had one other child, Edward, who was born in 1899. With only a limited education, Diamond quickly became street-smart, and by his teens, had become a thief.

Diamond's father moved his sons to New York City after his wife, Sara, died in 1913. John Diamond Sr. settled in Brooklyn, where he worked as a laborer. At the time, New York City was plagued by numerous gangs that attracted poor young boys to their ranks. Both John and Eddie Diamond became involved in a gang known as the "Hudson Dusters," which specialized in robbing packaged goods from delivery trucks. John Diamond quickly earned a reputation as an aggressive young thug. By the time he was seventeen, he had a long list of arrests for assault, burglary, and robbery. A few brief sentences at a reformatory school in New York did not convince him to lead a law-abiding life.

75

Diamond's criminal career was interrupted in 1918, when he was drafted to serve in the U.S. Army during World War I (1914-1918). After a very short time as a soldier, he went AWOL—absent without leave—an offense that was punishable by imprisonment. Diamond was soon arrested by military police, who delivered him to court. Tried and convicted of desertion, he was sentenced to five years' imprisonment in Leavenworth prison. Diamond was released in 1920, after serving only one year and one day of his sentence.

BACK IN BUSINESS

Shortly after his release, Diamond went to work for Jacob "Little Augie" Orgen, one of New York City's top racketeers (people that gain payments through various illegal methods such as fraud or violence) in the 1920s. Also in Orgen's gang were a number of rising stars in the New York underworld—such as Lucky Luciano, **Louis Lepke** (see entry), and Waxey Gordon. During the early years of Prohibition (when the Eighteenth Amendment outlawed the manufacture and sale of alcohol), Diamond and his brother, Eddie, worked in Orgen's bootlegging business, hijacking shipments of Canadian liquor that were being transported through upstate New York. Daring, calculating, and very good with a gun, Diamond quickly moved up in Orgen's organization. Together with his brother, Diamond took over much of Orgen's narcotics (drugs) and gem smuggling business.

Orgen was not the only gangster to stake a claim in Manhattan's profitable bootlegging business. In the early years of Prohibition, Joseph Weyler (known as Johnny Spanish), Nathan "Kid Dropper" Kaplan (who took the name of Jack the Dropper—or Kid Dropper—a boxer he admired), and Orgen fought for control of the same New York territory. On July 29, 1919, Spanish dropped out of the competition after he was murdered by Kaplan on his way out of a restaurant. With Spanish gone, Orgen and Kaplan battled for control of the enterprise.

A Plan to Eliminate Kaplan

Orgen enlisted Diamond to help him dispose of his arch rival. But Kaplan, who surrounded himself with gunmen, was not an easy target. A clever schemer, Diamond did not plan to commit the assassination himself. Instead, he convinced Louis Kushner, a small-time gangster, to do the actual dirty work. Kushner was being blackmailed by Kaplan and was eager to kill the man who was taking his money on a monthly basis. What's more, Diamond convinced Kushner that the killing would help him to move up in Orgen's organization.

The clay pigeon

Diamond was shot so often during his criminal career that he became known as the "clay pigeon [a shooting target] of the underworld." He survived so many shootings, that it was rumored that he was impossible to kill. The gangster reportedly boasted, "The bullet hasn't been made that can kill me." He was wrong.

Diamond came up with a plan that allowed Kushner to ambush Kaplan when he would have little opportunity to protect himself. First, he convinced a man named Jacob Gurrah Shapiro to file a complaint against Kaplan, who had assaulted him three years earlier. Shapiro had been wounded by Kaplan as he returned fire at Orgen's men in a battle that took place on Essex Street. The incident left two bystanders dead.

A Sitting Duck

Shapiro signed the complaint and on August 28, 1923, Kaplan was tried for the assault. Before he entered the courtroom, he was stripped of his gun, in spite of his objections that it was protection against would-be assassins. Diamond's plan fell in place exactly as he had intended. He knew Kaplan's whereabouts—and he knew he would be unarmed. Kaplan had become a sitting duck (easy target).

Kaplan left the West Side Court surrounded by policemen. He was led to the back seat of a squad car, where police captain Cornelius Willemse sat beside him. Kushner, who watched from across the street, crossed over to the car. Mounting the bumper on the back of the car, he fired several shots into the rear window, shattering the glass. The driver was wounded, but both Willemse and Kaplan were unharmed. Kaplan's wife attempted to stop Kushner as a crowd of police and onlookers watched. But Kushner pushed her aside, broke a side window in the squad car, and fired directly at Kaplan's head. The gang leader

Hard to find

Although Diamond boasted that he was impossible to kill, he made sure that he wasn't an easy target. He surrounded himself with gunmen who were loyal only to him. He also hid his whereabouts when he was visiting out of town by renting several rooms in the city—so that a gunman who wanted to kill him would not be sure where to find him. On the night of his death, Diamond slept in one of the several seedy (run-down) rooms he had rented in Albany, New York.

reportedly uttered "They got me" just before he died. Bragging that he had killed Kaplan, Kushner asked police for a cigarette and posed for newspaper photographers.

THE END OF "LITTLE AUGIE" ORGEN

While Kushner sat in jail, Diamond enjoyed his new standing in Orgen's gang. As a reward, he was given a large portion of the narcotics and bootlegging business that had belonged to Orgen's onetime rival. Diamond was not a modest man. A flashy dresser, he showed off his new wealth by purchasing expensive automobiles and lavish apartments. He became part-owner of a speakeasy (saloon) called the Hotsy Totsy Club, on the second floor of a building on Broadway between 54th and 55th Streets. And he showered money on his numerous girlfriends—one of whom was a chorus dancer named Marion Strasmick, known as Marion "Kiki" Roberts. (Although he was a married man, Diamond still had numerous affairs.)

Within a few years, Diamond had become a kingpin (chief) in the New York crime network as one of Orgen's most feared and trusted lieutenants. But in 1927, Orgen's reign came to an abrupt end. On October 15, he left his headquarters on the Lower East Side. Diamond accompanied his boss as his bodyguard. When the two approached a taxi, the cab door opened, and someone in the back seat opened fire with a machine gun. Orgen fell dead, with a dozen bullet wounds. Diamond was struck twice, but managed to drag himself down the street. After he arrived at Bellevue Hospital by ambulance, doctors announced that he had lost too much blood and would not survive his wounds.

But Diamond recovered—as he did many other times. He knew the men who had shot him and killed his boss. Louis Lepke and Jacob Shapiro—two young members of Orgen's gang who wanted to take over part of the business—had been the shooters. But Diamond refused to name the gunmen. He reportedly told police "Don't ask me nothin'! You hear me? Don't ask!

And don't bring anybody here for me to identify. I won't identify them even if I know they did it!"

AT WAR WITH DUTCH SCHULTZ

After he recovered from his wounds, Diamond made peace with Lepke and Shapiro by promising to stick with his original piece of Orgen's business—bootlegging and narcotics sales. He vowed not to attempt to claim any of his former boss's other rackets. But this agreement did not protect his claim to Orgen's bootlegging territory. **Dutch Schultz** (see entry), a powerful gangster, wanted to muscle in on Diamond's turf. Diamond and Schultz waged war for two years, until Joey Noe, Schultz's right-hand man, arranged for the two to discuss a truce (peace agreement).

In a meeting at the Harding Hotel, Diamond and Schultz discussed the particulars of a peace agreement. Diamond agreed to give Schultz the rights to the midtown beer territory. But he wasn't willing to give up the territory for free. Diamond reportedly collected $500,000 before the meeting ended. The peace treaty lasted only minutes. After Schultz and Noe left the Harding Hotel, two shooters opened fire on them. Noe was killed. When Schultz returned fire, the gunmen ran away. The war was on: Schultz swore that he would make Diamond pay for the ambush.

DIFFICULT MAN TO KILL

Diamond had already proved that he was a difficult man to kill. But his brother, Eddie, was an easier target. Schultz's gunmen traveled to Colorado, where Eddie was trying to recover from a lung ailment. Although he was ambushed in a hail of bullets, Eddie survived the shooting—only to die later of tuberculosis (a lung disease). Diamond was furious about the attack on his brother—the only person, some people say, to whom the gangster ever showed any loyalty. None of Eddie's attackers lived out the year.

Take a look at this!

The Roaring Twenties (1939) is considered to be one of the greatest gangster films of all time. Three World War I buddies find their lives cross unexpectedly in Prohibition-era New York. James Cagney plays a bootlegger who vies with Humphrey Bogart for the position of crime boss. Meanwhile, a friend, who has become an attorney, works to bring them to trial.

The room where Legs Diamond was shot: the window on the extreme right, one floor below the top.

ANOTHER BRUSH WITH DEATH

The war between Diamond and Schultz grew hotter. Diamond spent large sums of money to supply himself with deadly gunmen such as Salvatore Aricicio, Tony Fusco, John Herring, A. J. Harry Klein, Gary Scaccio, and Paul Quattrochi—as well as Joe McDonald, a deadly submachine gunner. The list of Schultz's men who had been slain by Diamond's artillery included James Ahern, James Batto, Antonio Oliverio, Moe Schubert, Harry Vesey, and Tom Walsh.

Schultz retaliated (struck back) by attacking Diamond himself. In October 1929, three of Schultz's men ambushed Diamond and his girlfriend, Kiki Roberts, at the Hotel Monticello as they dined in their pajamas. After they burst through the door they let loose a volley of submachine gun fire that ripped through the walls of the hotel suite. Roberts was unharmed. Diamond was shot five times—and lived.

In 1930, Diamond took a break from his feud with Schultz to travel to Europe on the *Baltic.* When he returned to New York he moved with his wife, Alice, to Acra, New York. In April 1931, as Diamond left the Aratago Inn, where they lived, he was shot several times in a drive-by ambush. Again he lived to tell about it.

The bodyguard

Diamond worked for a while as a bodyguard for **Arnold Rothstein** (see entry), the multimillionaire king of the rackets empire. He earned $1,000 per week for protecting his boss's life from hot-tempered gamblers who lost their money to Rothstein. Diamond was also expected to make sure that customers with a lot of money made it home safely—and he was in charge of "convincing" (forcing) gamblers who owed Rothstein money to pay off their debts.

A HOLLOW VICTORY

Several months after the shooting, Diamond traveled with some of his men to Albany, New York, to try to recruit two local bootleggers, James Duncan and Grover Parks. The two men wanted no part of Diamond's business—but the gangster's men convinced them to change their minds. Gary Scaccio and other members of Diamond's gang tortured the men by placing matches under their fingernails. They prodded them with heated fire pokers and cigarettes. Duncan and Parks eventually told Diamond they would work for him. But they went to the police to report the ordeal when they were set free.

CHARGED WITH KIDNAPPING

Diamond and Scaccio stood trial in Troy, New York, for the kidnapping. Notorious (well-known) for making promises he didn't plan to keep, Diamond let Scaccio take the blame—with the promise that he'd get him out of prison after a few months.

Hotsy Totsy murders

Diamond owned a speakeasy called the Hotsy Totsy Club with another gangster, Hymie Cohen. A popular spot among the gangster elite, the club was the site of many meetings—and more than a few murders. Many gangsters who were invited to the club for dancing and drinking left the establishment as corpses (dead bodies).

On June 13, 1929, a young crook named William "Red" Cassidy and some of his friends went to the club looking for trouble. Cassidy insulted the service and threatened Diamond and his enforcer, Charles Entratta. Diamond and Entratta shot Cassidy and his friend, Simon Walker, in front of the bar's customers and employees. Both men died.

Diamond and Entratta went into hiding—just long enough to take care of witnesses who could identify them as the killers. The two gangsters eventually surrendered, but they were released by the police because of "lack of evidence." None of the several witnesses were available to testify against the killers.

Diamond never made any effort to help Scaccio out of his ten-year sentence at Sing Sing prison.

On December 17, 1931, Diamond celebrated his victory in court with his friends and wife at a speakeasy in Albany. From there he went to visit his girlfriend, Kiki, in her apartment at 21 Broeck Street. He left after a few hours. Drunk, he ordered his driver, John Storer, to take him to a seedy boarding house at 67 Dove Street.

Sometime after Diamond fell asleep, a couple of men entered his room. As one of the gunmen held his head, the other shot him at point-blank range. Mrs. Wood, the landlady, heard the shots and called the police. When the medical examiner arrived, he pronounced Diamond dead.

WHO KILLED DIAMOND?

Although no one was ever convicted of Diamond's slaying, there are several theories about who killed him. Many assumed that Schultz's men had finally succeeded in killing their boss's rival. Others believed that Salvatore Spitale and Irving Bitz—two gangsters who had given Diamond money to set up narcotics connections on his trip to Europe—had ordered the killing after Diamond spent the money on himself. Still others speculated that the killers might have been hired by mobsters who feared that Diamond would try to take over their business—such as Lucky Luciano or **Meyer Lansky** (see entry).

Diamond's wife claimed to know nothing about the killing. In fact, she claimed that she didn't know that her infamous husband was a gangster. Alice Diamond was murdered two years later, in Brooklyn.

Diamond's girlfriend, Kiki Roberts, contacted the *New York American* after she learned of the gangster's death. She told reporters: "I was in love with Jack Diamond. I was with him in Albany, New York, before he was killed. But I don't know who killed him or anything about the murder." Roberts disappeared shortly thereafter. She later turned up—living under her real name, Marion Strasmick.

Sources for Further Reading

Nash, Jay Robert. *Bloodletters and Badmen.* New York: M. Evans, 1973, pp. 153–158.

Sifakis, Carl. *The Mafia Encyclopedia.* New York: Facts on File, 1982, pp. 107–108.

Who's Who in the Mafia. [Online] Available http://home1.pacific.net.sg/~seowjean/Mafia/mafia.html, November 7, 1997.

Diamond Joe Esposito
(Joseph Esposito)

Born: March 28, 1872
Died: March 21, 1928

Once a dirt-poor immigrant, Diamond Joe Esposito amassed a fortune by participating in bootlegging and racketeering ventures.

A BAKER ON THE MOVE

Esposito was born near Naples, Italy, in the small town of Accera. He grew up in poverty and immigrated to the United States in 1895, when he was twenty-three years old. Scrounging a living by taking whatever work he could find, he collected garbage, dug ditches, and carefully saved his money. After a few years he moved from Boston, Massachusetts, to Brooklyn, New York. At the age of thirty-three, he settled in Chicago, where he opened a bakery in the Nineteenth Ward, an area known as Little Italy.

Esposito continued to hustle, working odd jobs to supplement his income from the bakery. He worked for a while as a hod carrier—hard physical labor that required him to carry heavy loads of bricks to bricklayers and stonemasons. He soon organized his fellow workers into a union known as the International Hod Carriers' Building Construction Laborers' Union. Esposito was the union's treasurer and agent.

Esposito also helped establish the Circolo Accera Club, whose members came from his native village in Italy. As the club's president, he provided start-up money for a number of small businesses in the community—for which he collected a large share of the profits after the business was underway.

As the money rolled in, Esposito took care to improve his standing in the community. He threw expensive parties and helped to feed the poor. He donated money to help other Italians immigrate to America and he played Santa Claus during the Christmas holiday. Well before his fortieth birthday, Esposito had become a wealthy and influential man in Chicago's Italian community.

A BARBERSHOP BRAWL

Always heavily armed, Esposito was involved in a shooting in August of 1908. At the time, he and his barber, Mack Geaquenta, were dating the same woman. Esposito went to the barber shop for a shave and hair cut. As he sat in the barber's chair, with his face covered with lather, he began to argue with Geaquenta. The barber started toward him, but Esposito jumped up—his face still smeared with shaving cream—and pulled a gun. He ended the argument by shooting Geaquenta dead.

Esposito's trial did not take place until May of the following year. During the nine-month wait, the witnesses who had seen the shooting either lost their nerve or vanished. With no one to testify against him, Esposito was released.

DIAMOND JOE

Esposito was not a modest man. Fond of flashy displays of wealth, he was nicknamed "Diamond Joe" (or "Dimey"). A heavyset man who stood six feet tall, he wore a large belt with a buckle that spelled out his name with $50,000 worth of diamonds. He dressed himself in diamond rings, diamond cuff links, and diamond shirt studs (buttons). Like his friend, Big Jim Colosimo—who was also fond of diamonds—Esposito

Big trouble at the Bella Napoli

Many gangsters frequented Esposito's ritzy cafe, the Bella Napoli. Cuono Coletta, a well-known killer, was among the establishment's underworld clientele. One evening Coletta fired his gun in the cafe, blasting the tip off of one of Sam Esposito's fingers. Joe Esposito took grave offense at his brother's injury. One of Esposito's enforcers promptly shot Coletta in the head.

The police raided Bella Napoli in 1923 for serving wine illegally. The establishment was closed down for one year. Esposito was fined $1,000—a mild slap on the hand to a man as wealthy as Diamond Joe.

Deadly garlic

All of the bullets that were recovered from Esposito's body were reportedly dipped in garlic. Police believed that the murder might have been committed by Albert Anselmi and John Scalise, Al Capone's top assassins, who often dipped the tips of their bullets in garlic. They believed—mistakenly—that garlic-tipped bullets would poison their victims in case they survived the shooting. With fifty-eight bullets in his body, Esposito needed no poison to help him to his grave.

opened an upscale cafe. The Bella Napoli, on South Halsted, was a popular establishment, especially among gangsters.

In 1913, Esposito threw a three-day party to celebrate his marriage. He invited the entire Nineteenth Ward neighborhood (now the Twenty-fifth Ward) to the festivities, which cost the newlywed a whopping $65,000—$40,000 of which was for wine. Forty-one years old at the time, Esposito married a sixteen-year-old girl named Carmela Marchese.

POLITICS AND BOOZE

Esposito enjoyed a great deal of political clout (power). He was able to influence the voters in his neighborhood to the extent that he could guarantee political friends that the entire Nineteenth Ward would follow his lead. In 1920, when Esposito was forty-eight, his friend, republican Senator Charles S. Deneen, convinced him to run for a political office. In a landslide victory, Esposito won the post of ward committeeman.

Esposito celebrated his election by throwing a lavish party—even more extravagant than his wedding had been. Several people who hadn't been invited to the affair tried to crash the party. Esposito's enforcer, Tony "Mops" Volpe—one of Chicago's most ruthless killers—beat them up and threw them out.

At the time of Esposito's election, Prohibition (when the Eighteenth Amendment outlawed the manufacture and sale of alcohol) had gone into effect. Esposito, like many other gangsters, made a fortune by taking part in the bootlegging industry that produced, supplied, and transported illegal booze. Once in office, he appointed Volpe as the county's deputy sheriff. In so doing, he protected illegal liquor production operations he had installed throughout Chicago and the suburbs of Chicago Heights and Melrose Park.

Esposito employed thousands of illegal Italian immigrants, who worked for very low wages for fear of having their lack of U.S. citizenship exposed. The inexpensive hard liquor, beer, and wine that Esposito produced was delivered throughout the city—in spite of the efforts of Prohibition agents to turn Chicago into a dry (alcohol-free) town. Some of Esposito's enormous stills (machines used to make liquor) produced alcohol that bordered on poison. Esposito also supplied other bootleggers with the sugar to produce alcohol. The **Genna brothers** (see entry), who ran stills in the city, relied heavily on Esposito.

UNHEEDED WARNINGS

As rival bootleggers, the Genna brothers became embroiled (involved) in a battle with infamous gangster **Al Capone** (see entry). Esposito's loyalty to Capone angered the Gennas. To demonstrate their displeasure, they arranged the murder of two of Esposito's brothers-in-law. John Tucillo and Philip Leonatti were ambushed in a hail of machine-gun fire as they bought cigars. The murders were a warning to Esposito to abandon his allegiance (loyalty) to Capone.

Frank Nitti.

Esposito ignored the warnings and the Gennas were eventually destroyed by their rivals. By the spring of 1928, Esposito was on bad terms with Capone. Most of his underworld friends had been forced out of the business—or killed. On the morning of March 21, 1928, Esposito received a phone call from Frank Nitti, one of Capone's top aides. Nitti reportedly warned him, "Get out of town or get killed."

Again, Esposito ignored the warning. He suspected that someone was attempting to scare him off in order to take over his profitable businesses. Ralph and Joe Varchetti, Esposito's bodyguards, tried to convince their boss to retire to his farm on Cedar Lake where he could support himself raising chickens. But Esposito refused to leave his profitable rackets.

FIFTY-EIGHT BULLET HOLES

Later in the evening, Esposito walked toward his home on Oakley Boulevard with his bodyguards. A sedan approached the three men from the rear, and unleashed a round of machine gun fire. The Varchetti brothers survived. But Esposito, who took fifty-eight bullets in all, died on the spot. Ralph Varchetti later described the episode in court:

> Then there were more shots, and Joe says, 'Oh, my God!' and I knew he was hit. I dropped to the sidewalk and lay flat, with my face in the dirt. The shots came in bursts of fire from an automobile. . . . When the firing stopped a second, I looked up and they fired again. I dropped flat, and this time waited until they were gone. I got near Dimey [Esposito] and tried to wake him. He was gone.

The coroner's investigation produced no evidence to charge anyone with Esposito's murder. Esposito left behind a wife, who was then thirty-one, and three young children. His killers were never identified.

Sources for Further Reading

Nash, Jay Robert. *Bloodletters and Badmen*. New York: M. Evans, 1973, pp. 153–158.

Sifakis, Carl. *The Mafia Encyclopedia*. New York: Facts on File, 1982, pp. 107–108.

Who's Who in the Mafia. [Online] Available http://home1.pacific.net.sg/~seowjean/Mafia/mafia.html, November 7, 1997.

Louis Lepke
(Louis Buchalter)

Born: 1897
Died: March 4, 1944

One of several Jewish gangsters in the New York underworld, Louis Lepke rose to the highest level of the newly formed national crime syndicate (association). A multi-millionaire by the end of his career, he was eventually betrayed by fellow mobsters.

LITTLE LOUIS

Like many other gangsters who eventually rose to the top of the New York underworld, Lepke started out as a teenager robbing packaged goods from delivery carts in Manhattan. At the age of sixteen he was arrested for the first time. Lepke was so poor that, according to the police report, he wore stolen shoes. He got his nickname from his mother. "Lepke" is an affectionate Yiddish name meaning "Little Louis." But the gangsters who referred to him by his nickname did not do so with affection.

In the 1920s, during the early years of Prohibition (when the Eighteenth Amendment outlawed the manufacture and sale of alcohol), Lepke worked for crime boss **Arnold Rothstein** (see entry). While most other young gangsters of the era were involved in the profitable bootlegging business (illegal manufacture and sale of alcohol), Lepke decided to work in an area that had longevity—that is, an activity that would outlive Prohibition. Lepke chose labor racketeering (manipulating laborers through intimidation) as his specialty. Together with his boy-

A life for a life

Lepke was responsible for preventing the syndicate from ordering the assassination of Thomas E. Dewey, the New York district attorney who eventually became the governor of the state and a candidate for the U.S. presidency. Dewey knew nothing of Lepke's intervention at the time. Several years later, Dewey was largely responsible for building the criminal case against Lepke, which sent the racketeer to the electric chair.

hood pal Jacob Gurrah Shapiro, he joined the gang of "Little Augie" Orgen, who controlled labor racketeering in New York at that time.

UNGRATEFUL STUDENTS

Orgen trained Lepke and Shapiro in the rackets—and they were quick studies. Orgen's gang sold its services to both employers and unions in the garment industry—services that relied on muscle to put an end to labor strikes. Lepke soon grew restless. He wanted a share of his leader's business, and he wanted to have the freedom to explore many other racketeering opportunities that Orgen had ignored.

Orgen was aware that Lepke wanted a piece of the business for himself. He told his associates that he needed to put the young gangster in his place. But on October 15, 1927, as Orgen left his gang headquarters with his associate **Legs Diamond** (see entry), he was shot dead in a hail of machine gun fire that came from the back seat of a taxi cab. Lepke was the shooter. His friend Shapiro had been the driver.

A TAXING MAN

Lepke and Shapiro took over Orgen's rackets immediately. Although Orgen had offered strikebreaking services to both employers and unions, Lepke began to focus on labor unions. He helped local unions meet their demands by blackmailing (using threats to gain payment) employers. He also raised the fee for belonging to the union—and skimmed money from the dues members paid.

Lepke expanded his rackets empire to a number of other businesses. In exchange for payment, he offered "protection"—which amounted to nothing more than allowing workers to operate as usual. Bakery drivers had to pay a "tax"—one cent for each loaf of bread—to make sure that their bread was delivered before it became stale. Workers in numerous other businesses also paid Lepke's tax—from dry cleaners to poultry raisers, restaurant owners to shoe and handbag manufacturers. Lepke built a racketeering empire that pulled in some $10 million each year. Thomas E. Dewey, who eventually became governor of New York and a candidate for the presidency, referred to Lepke as the worst industrial racketeer in America.

MURDER, INC.

At the height of his career, Lepke was a member of the criminal elite that controlled the newly formed national crime syndicate. He acted as chairman of the board for the syndicate, which included Joe Adonis, **Frank Costello** (see entry), **Meyer Lansky** (see entry), Lucky Luciano, and **Dutch Schultz** (see entry) among its leaders. As such, Lepke—who was also known as Judge Louis—ordered the assassination of Schultz, who was being hounded by officials. A junior member of the board, Schultz had suggested that the gangsters arrange the murder of Dewey—who was at that time an aggressive special prosecutor—because he was putting too much pressure on Schultz's New York rackets. But Lepke realized that Dewey's murder would only make the situation worse by increasing police pressure on the gang's rackets. Schultz was murdered in 1935, in a restaurant in Newark, New Jersey, by a group of syndicate hit men.

Lepke—who had a reputation as a man who enjoyed hurting people—was also placed in charge of the syndicate's enforcement arm, which carried out the gang's violent activities. As the head of "Murder, Inc.," he was responsible for ordering and approving hundreds of killings. Lepke placed trusted associates in top positions in the organization. Shapiro, who had helped him ambush Orgen, was given a key role in Murder, Inc., as was another eager killer named Albert Anastasia.

LEPKE TAKES A POWDER

Dewey soon began to focus on Lepke's racketeering activities—particularly in the bakery business. At the same time, the federal government was investigating Lepke's involvement in restraint of trade (a form of racketeering). And the Federal

Working in Sing Sing

Even from prison, Lepke continued to influence the New York underworld. From behind the walls of Sing Sing prison, he ordered the execution of two of the men who had betrayed him. Abe Reles, the "canary" (person who informs on illegal activity) who tied Lepke to the murder of a candy store owner, was forced out of a window in a hotel on Coney Island. Moe "Dimples" Wolinsky—who had been instrumental in the double-cross that convinced Lepke to surrender—was shot to death in a restaurant in Manhattan.

Setting the record straight

On March 2, 1944, Governor Thomas E. Dewey issued a forty-eight hour stay of execution for Lepke, who claimed to have information that would reveal the criminal activities of a number of politicians. But the mobster wanted to make it clear to his associates that he would not inform on the syndicate's activities. He issued a statement through his wife:

> I am anxious to have it clearly understood that I did not offer to talk and give information in exchange for any promise of commutation of my death sentence. [A commutation changes a legal penalty to a lesser one.] I did not ask for that! The one and only thing I have asked for is to have a commission appointed to examine the facts. If that examination does not show that I am not guilty, I am willing to go to the chair, regardless of what information I have given or can give.

Lepke didn't need to worry about mob retaliation. He went to the chair on March 4, 1944.

Narcotics Bureau began to look into his role in large-scale narcotics (drug) smuggling. Lepke was arrested. Released on bail, he did not wait for authorities to arrest him on other charges. He went into hiding—staying in a number of different hideouts in Brooklyn. The federal authorities, who had no idea where to find the gang kingpin (chief), conducted a nation-wide manhunt.

Lepke's associates were not happy with the state of things. The gangster's disappearance had stepped up police pressure in New York—and throughout the country. The syndicate would not be able to return to business as usual until the authorities stopped searching for Lepke. Lucky Luciano—who ruled the mob from prison—was convinced that Lepke had to surrender. But Lepke faced the possibility of life imprisonment and would probably object to an order to turn himself in. So Luciano arranged for Lepke to be tricked into surrendering.

THE BIG FIX

Some of Lepke's trusted associates convinced him that the syndicate had "fixed" his problem. If he turned himself in, he would receive a light sentence with early parole—or so they said. Further, they claimed, he would not be prosecuted for his most serious crimes, which could easily land him in prison for life. Lepke agreed to surrender.

On August 24, 1939, Lepke surrendered. He met with Walter Winchell, a newspaper columnist who had repeatedly pub-

lished stories asking the gangster to contact him. Winchell delivered him to his friend, J. Edgar Hoover, who was in charge of the Federal Bureau of Investigation (FBI). Winchell reportedly introduced the two by saying, "Mr. Hoover, meet Lepke." Lepke realized immediately that he had been double-crossed by his associates. Hoover, who called Lepke "the most dangerous criminal in the United States," had no intention of showing leniency (tolerance) to the infamous racketeer.

Mrs. Louis Buchalter and her son, Harold, arrive at Sing Sing to visit her husband in his cell on death row, March 1, 1944.

DEATH ROW

Lepke received a fourteen-year sentence for his narcotics dealings, which had involved bribing U.S. customs officials. New York district attorney Dewey was responsible for adding another thirty-nine years to Lepke's imprisonment. But the worst was yet to come.

Dewey had begun to investigate the activities of Murder, Inc. Abe Reles, a former killer in the organization, made his job a great deal easier. In exchange for leniency, Reles informed on other members of the murderous association—including Lepke, who was responsible for the murder of Joe Rosen, a candy store owner who had once been a trucker in the gangster's territory in the garment industry.

In 1940, Lepke was taken from federal custody to New York to be tried for Rosen's murder. He was found guilty, along with two other gangsters, Louis Capone and Mendy Weiss. All three were sentenced to death.

NOT A PRETTY SIGHT

Lepke did not believe that his death sentence would actually be carried out. He had detailed knowledge of the involvement of politicians in syndicate activities—knowledge he hoped to use to his advantage. Lepke told newspaper reporters that he had damaging information about an important labor leader's involvement in criminal activities. "If I would talk," Lepke bragged, "a lot of big people would get hurt. When I say big, I mean big. The names would surprise you." Lepke's ploy worked for a while. He earned several stays (delays) of execution—including a forty-eight hour reprieve (postponement) that was granted on the day he was to be killed. But on March 4, 1944, his luck ran out.

Wealthy man in a hot seat Lepke--who was a millionaire many times over--is said to be the wealthiest man ever to have been executed in the electric chair.

Lepke ate his last meal—roasted chicken and shoestring potatoes—still convinced that he would receive a last-minute pardon. He was in good spirits until late in the evening. Burton B. Turkus, who prosecuted the Murder, Inc. case recalled: "Only late in the evening, with the final minutes of his life ticking away, did he slowly begin to realize that maybe he had relied on the wrong miracle-maker."

Shortly after 11 P.M., Lepke, Capone, and Weiss were escorted to the electric chair at Sing Sing prison. Capone went first. He was pronounced dead three minutes after he received the 2,200-volt shock. Weiss followed. Before he was fastened into the chair, he said, "All I want to say is I'm innocent. I'm here on a framed-up case. Give my love to my family and everything." At the warden's signal, the electric shock coursed through electrodes fastened on his head. In less than two minutes, he was dead.

Lepke said nothing before thrusting himself into the chair. According to reporters, his body jerked before becoming limp. His skin turned blue. One newspaper account of the execution concluded: "It is not a pretty sight."

Sources for Further Reading

Nash, Jay Robert. *Bloodletters and Badmen.* New York: M. Evans, 1973, pp. 85–90.

Sifakis, Carl. *The Mafia Encyclopedia.* New York: Facts on File, 1982, pp. 185–188.

Who's Who in the Mafia. [Online] Available http://home1. pacific.net.sg/~seowjean/Mafia/mafia.html, November 7, 1997.

Arnold Rothstein

Born: 1882
Died: November 6, 1928
AKA: Mr. Big, the Big Bankroll, the Brain, the Fixer, the Man Uptown

*Widely considered to be the father of organized crime in America, Arnold Rothstein was a tutor to a number of powerful mob bosses, including **Meyer Lansky** (see entry) and Lucky Luciano. Always operating in the background, he parlayed his mob activities into multiple millions.*

THE SON OF ROTHSTEIN THE JUST

Rothstein was born in New York City in 1882 to well-established immigrant parents. His family lived in a comfortable brownstone building on 47th Street west of Lexington Avenue. Rothstein's father, a respected Jewish merchant, was known as "Rothstein the Just" because of his fairness in business dealings. Having started with nothing, Rothstein's father eventually became so well trusted in the New York garment industry that he was called on to settle a labor dispute in 1919.

But Rothstein did not choose to follow in his father's footsteps. He left school at the age of sixteen, after having spent only two years at Boy's High School in New York. By the time he quit school, he was a gifted pool shark (someone who earns money by beating others at pool). Rothstein played in a pool hall that was run by John McGraw, the manager of the New York Giants. He also gambled compulsively—shooting craps (a dice game) in alleyways and playing poker with other hard-core gamblers. A math whiz, he was able to calculate odds in his head, and kept his skills sharp by adding, subtracting, and multiplying large numbers throughout the day. Rothstein's ability to calculate the odds of winning helped him to amass a small fortune before he reached the age of twenty. Just out of his teens, he became a co-owner of a lavish gambling house in New York, which reportedly earned him in excess of $10,000 per week.

Rothstein used his wealth to finance a loan-sharking business. He lent large sums of money to clients who repaid the loans—plus an outrageous interest payment (a fee that increased with time). Rothstein employed **Legs Diamond** (see entry) to collect the loans—using threats and violence to force reluctant clients to pay. But Rothstein discovered that it was in his interest not to force all of his clients to repay their debts. He lent large sums of money to politicians, police captains, judges, and other influential people whose favors were more valuable than cash.

Father crime

Rothstein was a pioneer in a number of criminal rackets. Although he remained in the background, he masterminded and bankrolled a number of criminal empires—including labor racketeering and narcotics smuggling. Because he thought in terms of a national crime syndicate (association), Rothstein has been called the "spiritual father" of modern organized crime.

THE BLACK SOX SCANDAL

Although his involvement was never proven, Rothstein was called the mastermind of the 1919 gambling fix that became known as the Black Sox scandal. Considered to be the greatest scandal in the history of American sports, the Black Sox incident involved the fixing of the 1919 baseball World Series, for which the Chicago White Sox became known as the "Black Sox." Eight White Sox players were bribed to throw—or lose—the first and second games of the series. Rothstein's associates, who had bet heavily on the White Sox's opponents, stood to make a fortune. Abe Attell, a featherweight boxing champion who worked for Rothstein, handled the bribing of the eight players: Eddie Cicotte, Oscar "Happy" Flesch, Chick Gandil, "Shoeless" Joe Jackson, Freddie McMullin, Charles "Swede" Risberg, George "Buck" Weaver, and Claude Williams. The bribes reportedly amounted to around $70,000.

Although Rothstein was publicly accused of the fix, no one ever proved that he was behind the bribery. In 1920, a grand jury convened (met) in Chicago to investigate the scandal. On

Quite a character

Writer F. Scott Fitzgerald created a fictional character who was based on Rothstein. The character, Meyer Wolfsheim, is described in *The Great Gatsby* as "a gambler . . . the man who fixed the World Series back in 1919."

The Park Central Hotel where Rothstein was shot was the site of another gangland killing. In 1957, Albert Anastasia was shot to death as he sat in a chair in the hotel barber shop.

the advice of his lawyer, William Fallon, he voluntarily testified before the grand jury. Rothstein immediately took an offensive approach, accusing the court and the press of treating him as a criminal. Although he never denied having been involved in the affair, he was never indicted (formally charged).

AN ENTERPRISING CROOK

Rothstein, like other members of the underworld, made a fortune during Prohibition (when the Eighteenth Amendment outlawed the manufacture and sale of alcohol). A shrewd (sharp) criminal, he claimed a portion of the bootlegging business (illegal manufacture and sale of liquor) that was both profitable and low risk. Working with associates in Europe, he imported liquor from distilleries abroad, where the manufacture of alcohol was legal. Rothstein purchased a Norwegian freighter to bring in whiskey from Scotland. His business was massive: the freighter imported twenty thousand cases at a time. Since other gangsters relied on Rothstein's shipments of liquor, he played an important role in bootlegging in New York—and therefore had little risk of being killed by his peers.

Rothstein used his vast wealth to help other bootleggers who were in trouble with the law. But he always did so for a price. Between 1921 and 1924, he put up an amazing $14 million in bail for liquor prosecutions. Of approximately 6,900 liquor-related cases during his lifetime, fewer than 500 went to trial without being dismissed. Through his political ties and police contacts—and vast sums of persuasive money—Rothstein became known as a "fixer" who could make any problem disappear.

Rothstein was also credited with changing the way that graft (illegal payments) was collected in New York. Prior to Prohibition, policemen had been responsible for collecting payoffs from politicians to gangsters. But this made the gangsters vulnerable to policemen who occasionally shifted their loyalty. Rothstein and his associates began to collect payoffs directly from the politicians—eliminating the policeman as middle man. When the gangsters wanted "favors" from the police department, they simply asked the politicians to see to their requests.

"The Great Mouthpiece"

Rothstein's lawyer, William J. Fallon-- who was known as "The Great Mouthpiece"--once said of his employer, "Rothstein is a man who dwells in doorways. A mouse standing in a doorway waiting for his cheese."

DEALING IN DRUGS

Rothstein knew that Prohibition would not last forever. And without Prohibition, the bootlegging business would disappear. To ensure continued success, he diversified (varied) his business investments. Rothstein bought nightclubs, gambling casinos, and racehorses. He fixed the odds on bets that he and his associates made, and when possible, he fixed the outcome. He was the mastermind behind a $1 million stolen-bond racket and he used blackmail (threats to gain payment) and violence to profit from labor racketeering (manipulating laborers through intimidation). He financed diamond smuggling. And he is considered to be the man who invented the modern narcotics (drug) industry.

Rothstein moved into the narcotics industry at a time when access to drugs was severely limited. Aware of a growing drug problem in American cities, Congress passed the Harrison Narcotics Act in 1914, which abruptly cut off the ready supply of cocaine, heroin, and morphine in the United States. By the middle of the 1920s, the market for illegal drugs far surpassed availability. Using his vast amounts of capital and political connections, Rothstein created a new system for the supply of narcotics. He bought drugs in Europe through legitimate pharmaceutical firms (companies that develop medical drugs), and then shipped his orders back home—while disguising the true nature of his shipment. Using his ties to various gangs throughout the country, he started a system to distribute drugs to a large network of gangsters.

A GAMBLING MAN

Throughout his life, Rothstein remained a compulsive gambler. He once said, "I always gambled. I can't remember when I didn't. Maybe I gambled just to show my father he couldn't tell me what to do, but I don't think so. I think I gambled because I loved the excitement."

In 1928, Rothstein took part in a two-day poker game that had been arranged by George "Hump" McManus. Also playing

Drug smuggling in disguise

To cover his drug-smuggling operation, Rothstein bought an import-export firm as a front--and, purely by accident, became a successful art dealer.

December 11, 1928. Police examine the files of Arnold Rothstein, in hopes of finding evidence to help solve his murder.

were two gamblers from California, Nate Raymond and "Titanic" Thompson. The game lasted for two days. By the end of the game, Rothstein owed $320,000. According to some stories, he tore up his IOUs (written promises to pay). According to another version, he claimed the game had been fixed and refused to pay. Whatever his reasons, Rothstein did not pay his $320,000 debt.

BETTING ON THE ELECTION

On November 4, 1928, Rothstein placed a large bet that Herbert Hoover, and not Al Smith, would win the presidential election. Also that day, he received a phone call summoning him to a room at the Park Central Hotel in New York. He informed his associates that he was going to see McManus. Thirty minutes later, a hotel employee found Rothstein at the foot of the service stairs. He had been shot in the groin.

Rothstein was taken to Polyclinic Hospital. He died two days later—on election day—before he was able to collect his $500,000 in winnings when Hoover was elected as president of the United States. Rothstein refused to name his killer.

A number of gangsters were suspected in the slaying. McManus was tried and released for lack of evidence. Raymond had an alibi (proof that he was elsewhere) at the time of the killing. Some people believed that rival gangster, **Dutch Schultz** (see entry), had planned the killing in order to take over Rothstein's rackets. And still others speculated that Legs Diamond had arranged the hit following a drug deal in which his employer double-crossed him. Rothstein's killer has never been identified. After his death, Rothstein's estate was appraised (valued) at almost $2 million. But no one knew the value of his hidden assets—which have been estimated at $50 million.

> **Here's a book you might like:**
>
> *The Great Gatsby,* 1925, by F. Scott Fitzgerald
>
> A vulgar, yet romantic wealthy young man crashes Long Island society in the 1920s and finds his heart captured by an impulsive and emotionally impoverished girl. Made into a movie in 1974 starring Robert Redford and Mia Farrow.

Sources for Further Reading

Jonnes, J. "Founding Father: One Man Invented the Modern Narcotics Industry." *American Heritage* (February-March, 1993), pp. 48–49.

Nash, Jay Robert. *Bloodletters and Badmen.* New York: M. Evans, 1973, pp. 475–478.

Sifakis, Carl. *The Mafia Encyclopedia.* New York: Facts on File, 1982, pp. 285–287.

Smith, Sherwin. "35 Years Ago." *The New York Times Magazine* (October 27, 1963), pp. 96–98.

Robbers

A gentleman stagecoach robber who left a poem at the scene of the crime. A murderous widow who lured bachelors to their deaths. A cigar-smoking lady bandit who enjoyed the celebrity of a star. A bank robber who reportedly broke out of prison using a wooden gun. These are just some of the robbers whose life stories you'll learn about in this section.

Was Ma Barker the vicious "she-wolf" that FBI director J. Edgar Hoover claimed she was? Did Belle Gunness die in the fire that burned down her farmhouse—or did the headless corpse found in the ruins belong to another woman? How was kidnap-victim-turned-robber Patty Hearst finally captured? What did Clyde Barrow have to say in his letter to automaker Henry Ford? And who was the infamous "Lady in Red" who informed FBI agents of the whereabouts of bank robber John Dillinger? The stories of the robbers covered here are filled with intrigue—and more than a few unanswered questions.

Ma Barker
(Kate Barker)

Born: 1871?
Died: January 16, 1935

To the FBI, Kate "Ma" Barker was the mastermind behind her sons' criminal careers. To her sons, she was a dowdy, middle-aged woman who liked the movies. In spite of these vastly differing accounts, one thing seems sure: she was a fiercely protective mother who was deeply attached to her sons.

ARIZONA DONNIE CLARK

Arizona Donnie Clark—who later became Kate Barker—was born to Scottish-Irish parents sometime around 1871 near Springfield, Missouri, in the Ozark Mountains. As a child she had once seen **Jesse James** (see entry), who was also a native of the area. The experience reportedly had a profound impact on her. The young Barker mourned the murder of James—who was, to many people, a folk hero like Robin Hood.

As a young woman, Barker played the fiddle, read the Bible, and regularly sang in church on Sundays. In 1892, she married a farm laborer named George Barker, who seemed to be resigned to a life of poverty. What is known about her married life is that it was hard, unhappy, and taken up with the raising of her four sons, Herman, Lloyd, Arthur (who was called "Doc"), and Fred. A wild bunch, the boys grew up in extreme poverty and soon fell into constant trouble with the law. Barker's loyalty to her children and the fierceness with which she protected them from the consequences of their delinquent

The fabulous Barker boys

Whether or not Ma Barker was a cold-blooded criminal is a question that will never be settled. But there's no doubt that her four boys were a nasty bunch.

Herman Barker. Born 1894. First of the Barker boys to get in serious trouble. Died in 1927 from a self-inflicted gunshot wound during a shootout with police.

Lloyd Barker. Born 1896. Sentenced to twenty-five years at Leavenworth prison for holding up a post office. Released in 1947. Worked at a gas station snack shop until 1949, when he was shot to death by his wife.

Arthur "Doc" Barker. Born 1899. Probably the gang's leader and deadliest killer. Sentenced to life imprisonment for killing a night watchman. Paroled. Captured on January 8, 1935 and sentenced to time at Alcatraz. Killed in January 1939, during an attempted jail break.

Fred Barker. Born 1902. Ma Barker's favorite son. Killed a police officer while attempting to steal a car. Fred died in 1935 with his mother during a shootout with FBI agents.

behavior, became something of a legend itself in the Ozark Mountains where they lived.

CONFLICTING IMAGES

As a historical figure, Barker is something of a puzzle. Never arrested for committing a crime, she was nevertheless suspected of being the leader of a gang that J. Edgar Hoover (1895-1972), director of the FBI, considered to be one of the deadliest of the era. Hoover portrayed Ma Barker as a cold-blooded woman. He once wrote that she was:

> . . . [the] most vicious, dangerous, and resourceful criminal brain of the last decade. . . . The eyes of Arizona Clark Barker always fascinated me. They were queerly direct, penetrating, hot with some strangely smoldering flame, yet as hypnotically cold as the muzzle of a gun. That same dark, mysterious brilliance was in the eyes of her four sons.

—**Persons in Hiding,** *published in 1938.*

But not everyone saw Ma Barker as the evil mastermind behind her sons' criminal activities. The public, fed on newspaper stories that detailed the escapades of her "boys" and their friends, perceived Barker as a mother whose love for her children was so extreme that it twisted both her conscience and her judgment. To the members of the gang, or so those who survived would later relate, she was no more than a simple-minded, middle-aged woman whose use to them was limited to her

Creepy Karpis

After his friends, Fred and Ma Barker, were killed in a hail of gunfire, Alvin "Creepy" Karpis (1907-1979) notified FBI director J. Edgar Hoover that he planned to kill him in the same way Hoover's agents had slain the Barkers. He never made good on his word, but he did manage to cause Hoover grief.

In 1935, Karpis robbed a train. This distressed Hoover, who saw the resurrection of this outdated crime as an insult to his professional reputation. When the FBI received information about the outlaw's whereabouts in May 1936, Hoover made certain that he was present at the arrest. As agents surrounded Karpis in his New Orleans hideout, the FBI director himself placed Karpis under arrest. Two years earlier, few Americans knew what the FBI was. And fewer still had heard of the agency's director Hoover. But by 1935, after the Karpis capture—and Hoover's supposed role in it—made headlines, Hoover and the FBI had become national institutions.

Hoover was praised as a hero and hard-hitting lawman. But Karpis told another story. He later wrote, "[Hoover] didn't lead an attack on me. He hid until I was safely covered by many guns. He waited until the coast was clear Then he came out to reap the glory. . . . That May day in 1936, I made Hoover's reputation as a fearless lawman. It's a reputation he doesn't deserve."

Karpis was sentenced to life imprisonment at Alcatraz, a brutal penitentiary on an island in San Francisco Bay, in California. In 1962, after twenty-six years at the institution known as "the Rock," Karpis was transferred to another penitentiary. Karpis endured more time at Alcatraz than any other man. Paroled in January 1969, he was deported (expelled from the country) to Canada, his birth country. Karpis, who once shared the leadership of the Barker gang, outlived all of the Barkers. He retired to Spain, where he died in 1979, at the age of seventy-two.

willingness to hide them from the law, raise bail money (money paid as a guarantee that an arrested person will appear for trial), or otherwise to secure their release on parole.

Alvin "Creepy" Karpis, who shared the leadership of the Barker gang, described Barker as a harmless—and even clueless—old woman. In his memoirs, published in 1971, he wrote:

> Ma was always *somebody* in our lives. Love didn't enter into it really. She was somebody we looked after and took with us when we moved from city to city, hideout to hideout.

Jelly Nash

Frank "Jelly" Nash—a bandit, bootlegger, and murderer—was one of the many outlaws who was given shelter by the Barkers. In 1924, Nash and a criminal named Al Spencer attempted to rob a mail train outside of Okesa, Oklahoma. The robbery was a failure. Nash was captured and sentenced to time in Leavenworth prison. He left the Kansas prison six years later—before he'd served his entire sentence. In prison, he worked as a cook at the warden's home. One day he simply strolled out the warden's back door. And he didn't leave empty-handed. He took an edition of William Shakespeare, an English playwright and poet, with him.

The rest of Nash's story was less poetic. The escaped train robber was later arrested at the White Front Pool Hall in Hot Springs, Arkansas. Federal agents took him to Union Station in Kansas City, Missouri, where he was to board a train headed toward Leavenworth. In the parking lot, three men ambushed Nash and the federal agents. Caught in machine-gun fire, Nash and four agents died.

It's no insult to Ma's memory that she just didn't have the brains or know-how to direct us on a robbery. It wouldn't have occurred to her to get involved in our business, and we always made a point of only discussing our scores when Ma wasn't around. We'd leave her at home when we were arranging a job, or we'd send her to a movie. Ma saw a lot of movies.

To the FBI, she was a criminal brain. To Karpis and others, she didn't have the know-how to direct a robbery. What, then, was the truth?

SPREE OF VIOLENCE

In the 1920s, Barker could no longer shield her sons from the law—or the punishments they received for increasingly serious offenses. Doc was arrested in Oklahoma for killing a night watchman during a burglary and sentenced to life imprisonment. In 1927, Herman was stopped by two officers outside of Wichita, Kansas, for questioning in connection with a recent robbery. Pulling his gun, he shot one of the policemen in the head. Herman was then shot by the other officer. Badly wounded and afraid of capture, Herman killed himself. Barker grieved for weeks afterward.

Struggling to find some motive for Barker's criminal activities, the FBI later explained that the death of her eldest child drove her into a vengeance-seeking spree of violence. According to Hoover, the incident caused Barker to change "from an animal mother of the she-wolf type to a veritable [genuine] beast of prey." She was reputed to have carried out a series of bank robberies and kidnappings unequaled in the history of modern crime. The truth was probably quite different, but by then it hardly mattered.

FUGITIVES AND NEW MEMBERS

After the death of Herman, little more was heard concerning the Barkers until 1932, the year Lloyd was arrested for mail robbery and sentenced to a twenty-five year term. Fred had been serving a term in prison for the shooting of a town constable (law officer) who had caught him attempting to steal a car. In 1933, under conditions that suggested his freedom may have been purchased, Fred was released and returned home to Barker in the company of Karpis. Fred was probably the first of the Barker brothers to form an alliance (relationship) with Karpis, who quickly became one of Barker's favorites.

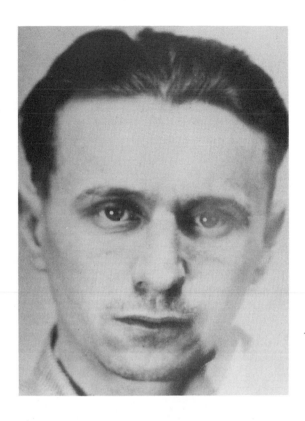

Ma Barker's favorite son, Fred, shown here in a 1934 mugshot.

The gang's membership was constantly shifting. At the time, Barker provided shelter to several wanted men, including Francis Keating (who was later captured by federal agents as he played golf), Frank Nash, an Oklahoma bandit and bootlegger, Al Spencer, a cattle rustler and bank robber who belonged to Henry Starr's gang, and bank robber Ray Terrill (whose gang was later destroyed after trying to rob two banks at once).

KIDNAPPED MILLIONAIRES AND A SILENCED GANGSTER

In a move that gave Hoover fits, the state of Oklahoma pardoned Doc, who promptly rejoined the gang and assumed, with Karpis, a leadership role. Shortly after Doc's return, Barker's

The arsenal of guns used by Ma and Fred Barker during their fatal standoff with federal agents on January 16, 1935.

lover, Arthur Dunlop, was killed. The gang suspected Dunlop of being an informant. A year later, in 1934, the gang reportedly gunned down George Ziegler, one of its own members.

In 1933, Ziegler had joined the gang. He was a veteran of World War I (1914-1918), a college graduate and engineer, and a gunman who had worked for Chicago mobster **Al Capone** (see entry). Ziegler, who had connections throughout the Great Lakes region, participated in two kidnappings engineered by the Barker-Karpis gang. In 1933, the gang abducted William Hamm, the founder of Minneapolis's largest brewery. (The FBI first accused gangster **Roger Touhy** [see entry] of Hamm's abduction.) Just six months later, they kidnapped Minneapolis banker Edward Bremer, for whom they received a $200,000 ransom (money paid for the release of a captive). Following the second kidnapping and ransom payment, Ziegler revealed the gang's participation to friends. He clearly posed a danger to the other members of the gang. Ziegler was murdered in Cicero, Illinois, on March 22, 1934.

While FBI agents searched Ziegler's belongings and tracked the leads they provided, Barker was sent to visit Ziegler's widow. She convinced the woman to turn over the money her late husband had hidden. FBI agents concluded that Barker was the brains of the Barker organization. It was a reputation that would outlive her.

The End of Ma Barker

By 1935, the Barker gang was doggedly pursued by the FBI. On January 8, Doc was captured by the special agent in charge of the FBI's Chicago field office, Melvin Purvis. Doc was captured without a struggle, as he was taking a walk—unarmed. Eight days after Doc's arrest, Fred was tracked to a rented cottage near Lake Weir, Florida, about fifty miles northwest of Orlando. On the morning of January 16, 1935, the house was quickly surrounded, and at the end of a six-hour gun battle both Barker and Fred were found dead.

Fred's body was riddled with fourteen bullets. But according to reports, Barker was struck by no more than three bullet wounds—and possibly only one. Some claimed that Barker had gone down in a blaze of gunfire as she fired a machine gun at the agents who surrounded the house. But if she had been firing at lawmen, she would have been in their line of fire—and would surely have received more than three wounds from the fifteen-hundred rounds of ammunition that were fired into the cottage. Some people speculate that Barker's fatal shot was not fired but lawmen—but by a woman who had just witnessed the death of her favorite son. The mystery of Barker's place in the gang was never solved, but the story of her death took a permanent place in the bandit lore of the day.

Sources for Further Reading

Nash, Jay Robert. *Bloodletters and Badmen.* New York: M. Evans, 1973, pp. 33–39.

Prassel, Frank Richard. *The Great American Outlaw, A Legacy of Fact and Fiction.* Norman: University of Oklahoma Press, 1993, pp. 282–283.

Sifakis, Carl. *The Encyclopedia of American Crime.* New York: Facts on File, 1982, pp. 51–53, 386.

Vandome, Nick, *Crimes and Criminals.* New York: Chambers, 1992, p. 15.

Black Bart
(Charles Boles)

Born: c. 1829
Died: ?
AKA: Charles Bolton, C. E. Benson,
Charley Barlow, T. Z. Spaulding,
and others

An older, distinguished gentleman, Black Bart robbed stagecoaches over an eight-year period in northern California and Oregon. Known as a robber who never harmed his targets, Bart sometimes left poetic notes to tease his pursuers. He was eventually caught and imprisoned. Released from prison early, he disappeared from the public eye.

FROM FARM FIELDS TO GOLD MINES

Charles Boles—who came to be known as Black Bart—was born in England around 1829. His parents, John and Maria Boles, were married on June 27, 1807, and had seven children—including Charles, who was their seventh child—before they left their native country for America. In the summer of 1830, the family left London on a boat that was bound for New York City. The family settled on a one-hundred-acre farm in Jefferson County, in rural upstate New York, near the St. Lawrence River. After they settled in New York, John and Maria Boles had two more children.

Not much is known about Boles's early life in the farming community of Jefferson County. Some historians assume that he was probably a good student. As an adult, Boles was well-spoken and well-read—and he had excellent penmanship (handwriting). At about the age of twenty, Boles left New York with his cousin, David Boles. They spent the winter in Van Buren County, Iowa, with Charles Boles's older brother,

William, who had settled there eight years earlier, in 1841. The following summer, Charles and David arrived in California, eager to seek their fortunes in the gold mines. Disappointed with their small success, they decided to return to New York. A little over one year after their arrival, in the fall of 1851, they returned East by ship. After months at sea, the Boles cousins arrived in New York in January of 1852.

But Boles wasn't cured of gold fever. Within three months, he was on his way back to the California gold rush. For two years, he panned (gold and gravel are separated by washing in a pan) and mined for gold—with little success. In 1854 he returned by land to New York no richer than he had started. But he had become very familiar with the layout of much of northern California, something that he would use to his advantage later in life.

A MAN OF IRON NERVE

After Boles returned to New York, he married Mary Elizabeth Johnson, probably in 1856. In 1857, they moved to the town of New Oregon in the northeastern portion of Iowa, near the Minnesota border. Boles's youngest brother, Hiram, had already settled there. On April 26, Charles and Mary's first child, Ida Martha, was born. Their second child, Eva Ardella, was born May 17, 1859. By 1861, Boles had moved his family to Macon County, near Decatur, Illinois. There, the couple's third daughter, Frances Lillian, was born on the sixth of June. Boles probably made his living as a farmer, as his father had—although it's possible that he was a schoolteacher.

The Boles's family life was interrupted by the Civil War (1861-1865). Within one year after the first shots were fired, Boles enlisted in the Union (Northern) Army on August 13, 1862. During his three-year term, he fought in seventeen battles and was injured three times, including a bullet wound in the abdomen near the hip. Having volunteered to join the army as a private, Boles became his unit's third highest-ranking soldier. By the end of the war, he had been promoted to first sergeant. He distinguished himself as a disciplined and courageous soldier. One of his fellow soldiers, a man named Christian Reibsame, said this about him:

> [He] was one of the bravest men in the regiment. . . . He was always at the front in every fight, and was wounded several times. He was a reticent [quiet] fellow, but was well liked. He was inclined to sport, and played a good game of poker. . . . He was a perfect specimen of a good soldier and a man of iron nerve.

After Boles returned from the war, he rejoined his family in New Oregon. They soon moved to Minnesota, where a relative of Mary's lived. There, the couple's fourth child, a boy named Arian, was born (probably in 1866). But Boles did not remain long with his family. On May 1, 1867, he set out to try again to strike it rich in the gold mines of the West. His family never saw him again. Although Boles wrote to Mary on a regular basis and spoke of a time when they would be reunited, he never returned home. After twelve years of regular correspondence, he suddenly stopped writing letters to his wife. His family assumed he was dead.

Quaker guns

Boles's experience in the Union Army during the Civil War might have helped him to formulate his battle-plan for stagecoach robbery. Both sides in the Civil War used "Quaker guns" (sticks that had been peeled and painted black to look like real guns) to deceive the enemy. Although Boles always worked alone, he sometimes convinced his victims that he was not alone by using a similar trick.

STAGECOACH ROBBER

Boles was far from dead. On July 26, 1875, a few miles east of Copperopolis, California, he committed a stagecoach robbery. It was the first in a series of successful holdups. At sunrise, as the four horses pulling the Sonoma-Milton stage were struggling up a steep section of road known as Funk Hill, Boles stepped onto the road—in front of the lead horse. He wore light-colored pants and linen duster (coat worn to kept dust off clothes). His face was covered by a flour sack that had holes poked through so that he could see. He also carried a double-barreled shotgun. Boles used this method in all of his robberies. The strange outfit disguised his identity and allowed him to startle the horses, so that they would ignore the stagecoach driver's instructions. And by stepping in front of the lead horse, he shielded himself from gunfire. (In fact, most drivers and guards didn't dare to shoot at him, even when they had a weapon. They didn't want to risk shooting the valuable lead horse.)

Driven by John Shine, the stagecoach held the usual contents: ten passengers, a U.S. mail pouch, and a Wells Fargo strongbox (a small safe). Boles ordered Shine to throw down the Wells Fargo box, but the driver hesitated. Boles then shouted, "If he dares to shoot, give him a solid volley [round of gunfire], boys." Seeing what looked like several shotgun barrels pointed at him from the brush, Shine threw down the strongbox as well as the mail pouch. After he ordered Shine to drive on, Boles broke into the safe and mail pouch, escaping with more than $300 in gold and cash. Shine drove a little way down the road and then returned to the scene of the crime. The masked robber was gone, but a half-dozen shotgun barrels were still positioned in the bush—or so it seemed. As it turned out, the "shotguns" were really sticks that had been propped up to look like guns.

A POET IN DISGUISE

No one had a clue who the masked robber was. Boles had a gentlemanly manner and appearance that didn't attract suspicion. He was well-dressed and very polite, with a mustache and graying hair that was receding at the temples. A fit man who was capable of hiking long distances, he was able to walk away from the scenes of his crimes—dressed as a hobo. In all, Boles committed between twelve and twenty-nine stagecoach robberies between 1875 and 1883. While he might have been given credit for some robberies he wasn't involved in, it's possible he wasn't blamed for others that he did commit.

In addition to his distinctive method of robbing stagecoaches, Boles added another "signature" to his crimes: he left a note of poetry behind. After his fourth robbery, on August 3, 1877, in Sonoma County, California, Boles left a note that was scribbled on a Wells Fargo ticket. It said:

> I've labored long and hard for bread
> For honor and for riches

Wells, Fargo & Company

In the nineteenth century, the U.S. government was not able to handle all mail delivery on its own. Private delivery companies took over some of the delivery responsibilities—for a price. In 1843, two men who had experience delivering freight, a Vermonter named Henry Wells and a New Yorker named William G. Fargo, combined their expertise to deliver freight and mail in Illinois and Ohio. Charging only six cents a letter—compared to the twenty-five cent fee charged by the U.S. Post Office—Wells and Fargo's company was a success. In fact, it was so successful that the government ordered them to stop undercutting its prices (charging a cheaper rate).

In July of 1852, after merging with another delivery company, Wells, Fargo & Company opened for business in San Francisco, California. Wells and Fargo's company became the leading mail deliverer, express agency, and bank in the West. The company ensured its position by taking over rival businesses—or forcing them to fail. In less than ten years, Wells, Fargo & Company had more than one hundred and twenty offices in the West, where people mailed anything from private letters to cash and gold dust. A large part of the company's business involved shipping gold bullion (gold still in raw or unrefined form) from California to mints (a place where the government makes coins) on the East Coast.

The express company used a number of methods to transport goods: it employed men on foot and horseback, mule trains, freight wagons, and steamers. The company also delivered shipments using stagecoach wagons—which soon became popular targets for robbers. During its most successful years, Wells Fargo maintained its own detective and police force in an effort to eliminate stagecoach robberies. It is estimated that Wells Fargo detectives captured nearly two hundred and fifty highway robbers, including Black Bart, who was probably the most successful Wells Fargo bandit ever.

> But on my corns too long you've tred
> You fine haired Sons of Bitches.

Each line of the poem was written in different handwriting, and it was signed "Black Bart, the PO 8." (Black Bart was a character from one of the robber's favorite books, and the PO 8 is probably a play on the word "poet.") Almost one year later, after his fifth robbery, Boles left behind a second poem. Inside the broken Wells Fargo safe was a poem that read:

> here I lay me down to sleep
> to wait the coming morrow

Boles committed his twentieth robbery in Yuba County, California, on December 15, 1881. The *Marysville Appeal,* a small-town newspaper, carried this account of the robbery written by George Sharpe, the driver of the Downieville-Marysville coach that was robbed.

"I was driving slowly up a bit of rising ground when suddenly a man jumped out from behind a tree by the side of the road and yelled 'Hold on there you . . . .' I pulled up the horses pretty quick and set the brake. Then I sat still and looked at the man. I had never been stopped on the road before, and was surprised-like. The man was about my size (pretty stoutly built and about 5 feet 10 inches high). His face was covered with white cotton cloth, but one corner of the cloth was torn so that I could see that his eyes were blue. He had on a long linen duster and a pair of blue overalls. On his head was a little whitish felt hat, with some light colored hair sticking through the crown. That's about all I remember of his looks."

perhaps success perhaps defeat
and everlasting sorrow.
Let come what will, I'll try it on,
My condition can't be worse,
But if there's money in the box,
It's munny in my purse.

—Black Bart the PO 8

Although a number of fake Bart poems appeared during Boles's lifetime, only these twelve lines are considered to be genuine.

THE HANDKERCHIEF CLUE

Boles's success as a stagecoach robber was unmatched. He continued to rob stages throughout northern California and Oregon—covering ten counties over a three-hundred-and- fifty-mile area. Usually he struck between June and November, taking a break from his profession during the winter months. He often returned to the scene of previous crimes: nine times he committed robberies within a few miles of earlier stick-ups. With more stagecoach hold-ups to his credit than any other robber, Boles—known only as Black Bart—was at the top of the Wells Fargo wanted list. The company offered a large reward for

He spoke in a clear, ringing voice, without any brogue or foreign accent. There was a double-barreled muzzle-loading shotgun in his hands. . . . I saw all these things in a good deal less time than it takes to tell about them. As soon as I stopped the horses the robber got back behind the tree so as to keep out of range of any guns that passengers might have. He kept his shotgun bearing on me from the word "Hold."

"Throw out that box," was his next order. I supposed he meant the Wells-Fargo box, but I didn't stop to make particular inquiries, and I threw it out on the side of the road towards him. . . . "Now drive on, you . . . ." he said. I drove on. . . . There was [a boy] on the box seat with me. He was badly scared. After I had driven on a piece, he said to me, "I'm glad that robber didn't get my parcel," showing me a little package wrapped up in a newspaper. "What have you in that?" I asked him. "I've got my lunch in it," he said. And that was all the poor little cuss did have in it.

his capture. Even so, Boles managed to slip away from the lawmen who pursued him.

On November 3, 1883, Boles's luck changed. He stopped a coach on a steep portion of Funk Hill, where he had committed his first robbery. But a young man with a gun—possibly a passenger who had gotten off the coach to hunt—returned to the coach as Boles was trying to open the strong box. He fired at the robber. Slightly wounded, Boles was forced to flee, leaving behind a number of personal items. When a posse (a group of people with legal authority to capture criminals) searched the area, they found a derby hat, a little food, flour sacks, a leather case for opera glasses—and a handkerchief. That handkerchief proved to be the undoing of Black Bart.

Wells Fargo had hired a number of detectives who were eager to collect the reward for the capture of Black Bart. The detectives attempted, with no success, to trace the opera glasses. They had better luck with the handkerchief, which had an ink laundry mark—FXO 7. Although there were over ninety laundries in San Francisco, the detectives managed to locate the laundry that used that identification mark. The handkerchief was soon traced to a man known as Charles Bolton, who had been living quietly in a boarding house in San Francisco. The man was in fact Charles Boles, who had informed his landlady

Military pension

Something about Charles Boles's background puzzles historians. As a soldier in the Civil War he was wounded three times, including a serious bullet wound to his stomach. His injuries should have qualified him for a military pension that would have provided him with money later in life. But Boles never applied for a pension, choosing instead to rob stagecoaches.

and others that he was a mining executive who was often called out of town to visit his mines.

At first, Boles protested that he was not a stagecoach robber. Finally, he confessed to *one* crime—the final robbery. In November 1883, he pleaded guilty to robbery, and was sentenced to six years in the San Quentin penitentiary (prison). After just over four years, when he was nearly sixty years old, Boles was released—probably because of his age. He promptly disappeared and a new rash of stagecoach robberies began. Following a holdup in November of 1888, James B. Hume, the chief of detectives for Wells Fargo, sent word to his detectives: "We have reason to believe that [a robbery] was committed by the notorious C. E. Boles . . . alias Black Bart." The detectives were never able to prove that he was involved in any robberies after his release. The date of Boles's death is uncertain, although a New York City newspaper mysteriously ran his obituary (death notice) in 1917. It's possible the death notice was real. On the other hand, it might have been written by the poet himself, who wanted the public—and lawmen—to believe that he was dead.

Sources for Further Reading

Adventure of Wells Fargo. [Online] Available http://wellsfargo.com/about/stories/ch3/, January 18, 1997.

The American West, A Cultural Encyclopedia, Volume 1. Danbury, CT: Grolier Educational Corp., 1995, pp. 121–122.

Collins, William and Bruce Levene. *Black Bart: The True Story of the West's Most Famous Stagecoach Robber.* Mendocino, CA: Pacific Transcriptions, 1992.

Nash, Jay Robert. *Bloodletters and Badmen.* New York: M. Evans, 1973, pp. 61–62.

Prassel, Frank Richard. *The Great American Outlaw, A Legacy of Fact and Fiction.* Norman, OK: University of Oklahoma Press, 1993, pp. 123–125.

Bonnie and Clyde

(Bonnie Parker and Clyde Barrow)

Bonnie Parker: 1911-1934
Clyde Barrow: 1909-1934

Romanticized for their devotion to each other and their devil-may-care lives on the run, Bonnie Parker and Clyde Barrow were headline-makers. They robbed banks and stores—but not very successfully. They killed—with no sign of remorse. And they captured the public's imagination—both then and now.

BONNIE MEETS CLYDE

Clyde Barrow was born in Telice, Texas, on March 24, 1909. His parents, Henry and Cumie Barrow, had seven other children. The Barrow family was extremely poor. As a youth, Barrow was sent to the Harris County School for Boys, a reformatory, where he was deemed to be "an incorrigible truant [absent from school without permission], thief, and runaway." After he was released, Barrow joined a gang of petty thieves in Houston, Texas, known as the Square Root Gang. While still in his teens, he joined his older brother Ivan Marvin "Buck" Barrow in stealing cars and robbing grocery stores and gas stations.

In 1928, after the pair robbed a gas station in Denton, Texas, police pursued the Barrow brothers in a high-speed chase. Buck Barrow was shot and severely wounded during the chase. Although he was a skilled driver, Clyde eventually crashed into a ditch. He left his bleeding brother behind, possibly to ensure that he received needed medical attention. Buck Barrow received a

121

Car talk

Barrow once wrote a letter to automobile manufacturer Henry Ford (1863-1947). "I have drove [driven] Ford's exclusively when I could get away with one. For sustained speed and freedom from trouble, the Ford has got every other car skinned." Barrow concluded by adding, "even if my business hasn't been strictly legal it don't hurt anything to tell you what a fine car you got in the V-8 [a car with an eight-cylinder engine] ." Barrow and Parker took pictures of each other posing with their pride and joy, a 1932 V-8 they had stolen in Texas.

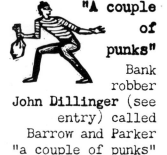

"A couple of punks" Bank robber **John Dillinger** (see entry) called Barrow and Parker "a couple of punks" who gave bank robbing a bad name.

five-year sentence at the Eastham prison farm, while his brother remained at large.

Less than two years later, Barrow met a woman who would change his life. Bonnie Parker was the daughter of a modestly well-off family from the farming community of Rowena, Texas. At the age of sixteen, she married a schoolmate, Roy Thornton. After Thornton was sentenced to a life term in prison for murder, Parker became restless. In 1930, she moved to Dallas, Texas, where she took work as a waitress. She later described her state of mind at the time as "bored crapless." That is, until Barrow walked into her life. Later that month, Parker met Barrow at the cafe where she worked. The pair immediately became inseparable.

BURNING HELL

Parker and Barrow moved in together and tried, for a while, to earn an honest living. Soon, however, Barrow was arrested for a burglary in Waco, Texas. There was no denying the crime: Barrow had left his fingerprints at the scene. He was sentenced to two years in a Waco jail.

Before long, Barrow walked out of jail brandishing the revolver Parker had smuggled to him during a visit. But Barrow's freedom was short lived. In Middleton, Ohio, police arrested him. An escaped convict, Barrow received a harsh sentence. He was sent a prison known as "the Burning Hell"—the Eastham prison farm.

Prison conditions at Eastham were savage. Barrow was whipped and forced to withstand vicious punishments. Brutalized by the experience, he became a more hardened criminal during his imprisonment. Barrow reportedly killed his first victim while in prison—a man named Ed Crowder, who informed prison authorities that Barrow had been gambling.

Barrow's mother, Cumie Barrow, fought to have her son released from Eastham. In January 1932, she visited Texas governor Ross Sterling to ask him to pardon her son. On February 2, 1932, Barrow walked away from Eastham—vowing that he would die before he ever returned to prison.

ROBBERIES AND KILLINGS

Barrow returned to Parker—and criminal activity—after his release from prison. The two committed a number of robberies until the police caught up with them during a botched theft. According to one story, after their car broke down while they were attempting to escape, Barrow and Parker attempted to "flee" on mules. Although Barrow escaped, Parker was captured in Mabank, Texas. It was an unusual situation, because Barrow was fiercely loyal to Parker. During the couple's many encounters with police, he often fought to help her to escape, risking his own capture.

During Parker's absence, Barrow committed several more robberies, killing two law officers in Atoka, Oklahoma. It was the first time he had killed lawmen, but it would not be the last. Shortly after Parker returned, the couple hooked up with Ray Hamilton, a gun-crazy thief and killer. The three robbed small banks and stores, killing lawmen and others. Hamilton eventually left the criminal company of Barrow and Parker, but he continued to commit crimes. In 1935, after having escaped from jail a number of times, he was put to death in the electric chair.

WANTED KILLERS

Buck Barrow walked out of prison after Miriam "Ma" Ferguson, the governor of Texas, granted him a pardon. Following his release, Buck rejoined Parker and his younger brother, bringing his wife, Blanche, with him.

In Joplin, Missouri, police surrounded the house the outlaw's were living in. A shootout followed, leaving two policemen dead, but the four criminals escaped.

The incident marked a turning point for Barrow and Parker. After police found photographs that the fugitives left behind,

The ballad of Bonnie and Clyde

On the day that Barrow and Parker were killed, the news of their death received front-page coverage in Dallas, Texas, newspapers. The *Daily Times Herald* printed a long poem about Bonnie and Clyde, claiming that it "came into the hands of the *Daily Times Herald* several months ago with the understanding that it was not to be released until the death of the Parker girl." In many ways, the poem, which was written by Parker, accurately foretold the death of Bonnie and Clyde:

You have heard the story of Jesse James,
Of how he lived and died.
If you still are in need
of something to read,
Here is the story of Bonnie and Clyde.
Now Bonnie and Clyde are the Barrow gang.
I'm sure you all have read
How they rob and steal,
And how those who squeal,
Are usually found dying or dead.
There are lots of untruths to their write-ups,

They are not so merciless as that;
Their nature is raw;
They hate all the laws,
The stool-pigeons, spotters and rats.
They class them as cold-blooded killers,
They say they are heartless and mean, But
    I say with pride,
That I once knew Clyde
When he was honest and upright and clean.
But the law fooled around, kept tracking
    him down,
And locking him up in a cell,
Till he said to me,
"I will never be free,
So I will meet a few of them in hell."

This road was so dimly lighted
There were no highway signs to guide,
But they made up their mind
If the roads were all blind
They wouldn't give up till they died.

The road gets dimmer and dimmer,
Sometimes you can hardly see,

their pictures were printed nationwide. *The New York Times* wrote about them. Newspapers and wanted posters provided physical descriptions, photographs, and information about their relatives. Bonnie and Clyde had gone public.

In November 1932, a gas-station attendant, William Daniel Jones, joined the outlaws—after they kidnapped him during a robbery. At first, he willingly joined them in robberies. But he

Still it's fight, man to man,
And do all you can,
For they know they can never be free.
If they try to act like citizens,
And rent them a nice little flat,
About the third night
They are invited to fight,
By a submachine gun rat-tat-tat.
If a policeman is killed in Dallas
And they have no clues to guide—
If they can't find a fiend,
They just wipe the late clean,
And hang it on Bonnie and Clyde.
Two crimes have been done in
    America
Not accredited to the Barrow mob.
For they had no hand
In the kidnapping demand,
Or the Kansas City depot job.

A newsboy once said to his buddy:
"I wish old Clyde would get jumped;
In these awful hard times,
We'd make a few dimes,
If five or six cops would get bumped."

The police haven't got the report yet,
Clyde sent a wireless today
Saying, "We haven't a peace flag of white
We stretch out at night,
We have joined the NRA."

They don't think they're too tough or
    desperate,
They know the law always wins,
They have been shot at before,
But they do not ignore,
That death is the wages of sin.
From heartbreaks some people have
    suffered,
From weariness some people have died,
But take it all in all,
Our troubles are small,
Till we get like Bonnie and Clyde.
Some day they will go down together,
And they will bury them side by side.
To a few it means grief,
To the law it's relief,
But it's death to Bonnie and Clyde.

later described the time he spent with the Barrow gang as "eighteen months of living hell."

The band of outlaws went on a crime spree that spread from Texas into Iowa. None of their robberies was highly successful: they never collected more than $3,500. But what they lacked in profits they made up for in violence. By the end of their criminal careers, Barrow and Parker were blamed for the deaths of at least twelve people.

A NARROW ESCAPE

In July 1933, their luck began to fail. Hiding at an empty fair grounds, the outlaws were surprised by police. Buck was fatally wounded, and Blanche was captured. The remaining gangsters managed to escape—although Parker and Jones had been wounded. Shortly after the incident, Jones left Barrow and Parker, and was later sent to prison.

The outlaw couple continued their spree of violence. Within a few months, four more law officers were dead. In January 1934, they pulled a daring prison break to free their former partner, Ray Hamilton. During the raid they freed another prisoner, a convict named Henry Methvin. The incident only increased the pressure on the fugitives, who were now pursued by a special squad of lawmen headed by Frank Hamer, a captain in the Texas highway patrol and former Texas Ranger. Hamer's sole responsibility was to locate the notorious couple.

DEATH TO BONNIE AND CLYDE

Barrow and Parker avoided capture until May 23, 1934. The couple drove down a backroad near Arcadia, Louisiana, to meet Methvin, with whom they had arranged a meeting. Parker ate a sandwich. Barrow sat in the driver's seat of the stolen Ford V-8, wearing only socks on his feet. Methvin was nowhere near the appointed meeting spot: he had sold them out.

In exchange for leniency, Methvin had informed police where to find Barrow and Parker. With five other lawmen, Hamer created an ambush post near the supposed meeting spot. Hidden from view, the posse (a group of people with legal authority to capture criminals) waited with rifles and shotguns. When the outlaws' gray Ford approached, the lawmen fired. Both Barrow and Parker died on the spot. Their bodies were riddled with bullets: Barrow had received twenty-five bullet wounds, while Parker had twenty-three.

Inside the outlaws' car, police found an arsenal of weapons. They recovered two Browning shotguns, three Browning rifles,

one revolver, eight automatic pistols, and more than two thousand rounds of ammunition. A large crowd gathered at the scene of the killings. Souvenir hunters reportedly tore bits of clothing from the victims, and cut locks of Parker's hair. They also chopped trees to get at bullets and picked up bits of shattered glass.

It's unlikely that Barrow and Parker would have surrendered to the police. But it's unclear whether they were ever given the chance to do so. In any case, the ambush received official approval. Thomas L. Blanton, a Texas congressman, later said "Hamer's method is the quickest and most effective way of disposing of them. We do not capture alive and try rattlesnakes. We shoot their heads off before they strike."

The bullet-riddled car that Bonnie and Clyde died in.

Grave words

Parker's tombstone was engraved with a poem:

As the flowers are all made sweeter
By the sunshine and the dew,
So this old world is made brighter
By the lives of folks like you.

Not everyone agreed with the gravestone's sentiments.

POST MORTEM

Reporters rushed to interview members of the victims' families. On the day of the shootings, the *Dallas Daily Times Herald* printed their reactions. Parker's mother fainted when she heard the news, while Cumie Barrow questioned, "Mister, is my son really dead?" The following day, the same newspaper ran a story in which Parker's aunt said, "I am glad she is dead," adding that her niece was "surely in hell." Blanche Barrow, Clyde's sister-in-law, was quoted in the same story as saying, "I'm glad they were both killed. It was the easiest way out." Captain Hamer felt similarly. He later said, "I never had the slightest regret. I never killed anyone except human vermin that deserved killing. . . . I hate to have to shoot her, but, as they drove up that day and I pulled down on Barrow, knowing that some of my rifle bullets were going to snuff out her life along with his, I recalled how she had helped Barrow kill nine peace officers . . . you can't afford to feel mercy for such murdering rats, whether they are male or female."

While the bodies of Barrow and Parker rested inside a funeral home in Dallas, twenty thousand people waited outside. Some offered to donate money to purchase wreaths of flowers for their funerals. Hot dog vendors set up stands to feed the crowds of onlookers. Barrow and Parker were buried separately, at the request of Parker's mother. Barrow was buried next to his brother in West Dallas cemetery, while Parker was interred at Fish Trap Cemetery. (She was later taken to Crown Hill Memorial Park.)

Sources for Further Reading

Bruns, Roger. *The Bandit Kings From Jesse James to Pretty Boy Floyd.* New York: Crown, 1995, pp. 168-169.

Nash, Jay Robert. *Bloodletters and Badmen.* New York: M. Evans, 1973, pp. 39-45.

Prassel, Frank Richard. *The Great American Outlaw, A Legacy of Fact and Fiction.* Norman: University of Oklahoma Press, 1993, pp. 297-300, 342-344.

Sifakis, Carl. *The Encyclopedia of American Crime.* New York: Facts on File, 1982, pp. 85-87.

Vandome, Nick. *Crimes and Criminals.* New York: Chambers, 1992, pp. 32-33.

Margie Dean

Born: 1896
Died: 1918

*Although a minor criminal, Margie Dean is remembered as one of the first getaway drivers in the history of bank robbery in the United States. Killed in her car during a shootout with police, she died just as **Bonnie and Clyde** (see entry) did—some sixteen years earlier.*

A GETAWAY DRIVER

Dean was born Margie Cellano in a ghetto in Paris, France, in 1896. As a young girl she emigrated to New York City and quickly turned to shoplifting. Having left New York City for Chicago, Illinois, she was arrested for stealing diamonds from a jewelry store. While serving out her sentence at Joliet Penitentiary in Illinois, she met inmate Eva Lewis, who was a member of a criminal gang headed by Frank "Jumbo" Lewis and Dale Jones. After they were released from prison, Dean and Lewis joined the gang of bank robbers, which also included Roscoe Lancaster and ex-convict Roy Sherrill. Dean quickly took a liking to gang leader Jones, and the two were eventually married. (It is unknown how she ended up with the name "Dean.")

Using Dean as their getaway driver, the Lewis-Jones Gang robbed banks throughout the Midwest. A skillful driver, Dean kept the car running while her fellow gangsters held up the bank. As the robbers fled, she let them into the car and raced out of town before police or investigators had a chance to trail them. The Lewis-Jones Gang is considered to be responsible for mastering the art of the automobile getaway.

THE MYSTERIOUS MRS. FORBES

On September 24, 1918, the gang's luck began to run out. Pursued by the Kansas City, Missouri, police, Dean, Jones, and Lancaster were trapped together in a house on Mount Gall Avenue. Surrounded, they attempted to shoot their way out of the house. Dean and Jones managed to slip out as Lancaster shot at the police who were charging through the front door. After wounding two officers, he was fatally wounded. Just before dying, Lancaster reportedly told police, "Jones is nuts! He wants to get in the movies."

Lancaster's statement helped police track the fugitive couple. Police and Pinkerton (a famous detective agency) detectives focused on Los Angeles, California—near Hollywood, the center of the nation's fledgling movie-making industry. The Pinkerton detectives had been investigating the gang for some time. Due to careful research, they knew that Dean liked one brand of perfume in particular. With the help of the owner of an upscale perfume shop in Los Angeles, detectives located a woman, who used that particular perfume, who called herself "Mrs. Forbes."

Herman K. Lamm, bank robber extraordinaire

Although the members of the Lewis-Jones Gang were innovative bank robbers, they were not very successful. One of the greatest daylight bank robbers of all time was Herman K. Lamm. Although daylight bank robberies were common in the western states in the 1800s, few East Coast robbers ventured into banks during business hours with the intention of withdrawing money illegally. That is, until Lamm came along.

A former Prussian army officer, Lamm carefully plotted his robberies. He made a floor plan of his target and memorized it. He staged fake robberies with his crew in order to practice every movement, and he mapped out an escape route in mind-boggling detail. The dashboard of the getaway vehicle contained detailed descriptions of the roads and notes about other possible routes. "The Baron," as he was called, was an expert driver who had car racing experience. He even tested his escape routes in bad weather conditions to determine how long it would take to reach his destination.

Lamm's career lasted more than a dozen years—much longer than the average bank robber's lifespan as a criminal. He was killed in 1930, but his legend did not end there. Two of Lamm's associates joined forces with a group of men who would later form the ranks of **John Dillinger**'s (see entry) gang. The gangsters met in prison. Dillinger's men allowed the bank robbers to take part in their prison break on one condition: they had to reveal their methods for successful bank heists.

The getaway car

The Lewis-Jones Gang has been given credit for perfecting the use of the getaway car in bank robberies. Before the introduction of the automobile, bank robbers had to flee on foot or on horseback—both of which were risky means of escape. With Dean posted outside the bank in an idling car, the Lewis-Jones robbers had a leg up on pursuing policemen.

LEADED GAS

Police and detectives staked out Mrs. Forbes's address on November 24, 1918. What they saw at the small house on Sierra Madre Avenue confirmed their suspicions: Dean was, in fact, Mrs. Forbes. After Dean and Jones drove away from the house, two police cars followed them. The gangsters stopped at a gas station in Arcadia, a suburb of Los Angeles. Before they were able to refuel their car, the police pulled in behind them.

A fierce gun battle followed. Dean fired at the police with a shotgun that rested on a swivel, while Jones pulled out an automatic weapon. Deputy Sheriff George Van Vliet was struck in the face by Dean's shotgun fire—and was blasted clear out of his car. The police fired back. Surrounded by twelve officers, Dean and Jones died as their car was hammered by gunfire.

Sources for Further Reading

Nash, Jay Robert. *The Encyclopedia of World Crime.* Wilmette, IL: Crime Books, 1990, p. 891.

Nash, Jay Robert. *Look for the Woman: A Narrative Encyclopedia of Female Poisoners, Kidnappers, Thieves, Extortionists, Terrorists, Swindlers, and Spies from Elizabethan Times to Present.* New York: M. Evans, 1981, pp, 117–118.

Sifakis, Carl. *The Encyclopedia of American Crime.* New York: Facts on File, 1982, pp. 47–48.

John Dillinger

Born: June 22, 1903
Died: July 22, 1934

Dillinger liked to say that he robbed banks, not people. Known as "Gentleman Johnnie," he was said to have been pleasant—and often flirtatious—during his many bank robberies. Although there is no evidence that he ever killed anyone, he became the subject of what was at the time the greatest manhunt in American history.

RAISED IN INDIANA

John Herbert Dillinger was born in Indianapolis, Indiana, in 1903. Four years later, his mother, Mollie, died. His father, John Wilson Dillinger, a grocer, was left to raise his son and fifteen-year-old daughter, Audrey. In 1912 Dillinger's father married Elizabeth Fields, who was from Mooresville, a farming community about twenty miles southwest of Indianapolis. When Dillinger was eleven years old, his half-brother, Hubert Dillinger, was born. Two year's later, in 1916, his half-sister, Doris, followed.

Dillinger's early life was quite normal. As a student, his grades were better than average. An outstanding athlete, he enjoyed playing baseball. He sometimes worked in his father's store, and was well liked by his neighbors. But Dillinger eventually became involved with a youth gang known as the Dirty Dozen. As a member of the gang, he was charged with stealing coal from carts belonging to the Pennsylvania Railroad, and selling the stolen coal to neighbors. He was in the sixth grade

The man who stopped Dillinger

In 1934 Melvin Purvis (1903–1960), special agent in charge of the FBI's office in Chicago, received word that the nation's most notorious bank robber, John Dillinger, had driven a stolen car across a state line, a violation of federal law, to make good his escape from an Indiana jail. Purvis and the bureau's efforts to locate and apprehend America's "Public Enemy Number One" were closely followed by both press and public for some four months—a chase filled with all the melodrama of an exciting and violent adventure story. On July 22, acting on a tip, Purvis and a squad of agents shot Dillinger as he reportedly attempted to resist capture outside a movie theater in Chicago. Later that year, Purvis was voted eighth in a poll of the year's outstanding world figures conducted by *Literary Digest*.

Dillinger was not the only criminal whose career was cut short by special agent Purvis. He was in charge of the manhunts that stopped Pretty Boy Floyd, Baby Face Nelson, Thomas H. Robinson Jr., and Verne Sankey. The prestigious *New York Times* once praised the famous G-man as the downfall of public enemies.

A Career Filled with Ups and Downs

Purvis was born in Timmonsville, South Carolina, to a plantation family. He earned a law degree from the University of South Carolina in 1925 and practiced for two years before joining the Department of Justice. Prior to his appointment as special agent in charge of the Chicago office, Purvis served in the FBI's field offices in Dallas, Texas, and Kansas City, Missouri. In 1932, after five years of service in various field offices, he was assigned to Chicago. There he was charged with capturing Dillinger—dead or alive.

Purvis's career was punctuated by a number of devastating failures. In 1933, he arrested **Roger Touhy** (see entry) and three others for the kidnapping of William Hamm, a St. Paul, Minnesota, millionaire. Soon after Touhy was cleared of that kidnapping, Purvis arrested the gangster for the kidnapping of Jake "the Barber" Factor. Although Touhy was sentenced to ninety-nine years in prison, it was later revealed that he

when he was taken to court for his first offense. Soon afterward, Dillinger's father bought a farm in Mooresville.

A STIFF SENTENCE

Shortly after his twentieth birthday, Dillinger enlisted in the U.S. Navy—possibly to avoid being arrested for having stolen a car. He completed basic training and was assigned to work as a

had not been involved in the incident. The kidnapping had been engineered by the Capone mob, which had manipulated the bureau to rid itself of a rival.

The manhunt for Dillinger, too, had encountered disaster. In April 1934, Purvis set a trap to ambush the gangster at the Little Bohemia resort in Wisconsin. The incident, which failed to deter Dillinger, left one innocent man dead and two others wounded. Reacting to the disaster, newspapers urged the FBI to terminate Purvis. But director J. Edgar Hoover refused to accept Purvis's resignation. If Hoover had accepted it, it would have tarnished the bureau's already troubled image.

Trouble with His Boss

Purvis's career was marked by conflict with Hoover, his superior. Throughout the country, the Bureau's field offices sent out press releases that began, "J. Edgar Hoover announces. . . ." But not in Chicago. Special agent Purvis took credit for news from the regional office—a bold practice that did not sit well with the FBI director. Hoover reportedly played a role in Attorney General Homer Cummings's decision not to allow Hollywood to produce a movie about the special agent's career.

The tug-of-war between Purvis and Hoover did not end when Purvis resigned from the FBI in July 1935 "for personal reasons." The situation was such that Hoover issued a statement to deny that he and the special agent had fallen out. But when Purvis took a job as the announcer of the *Post Toasties Junior Detective Corps*—a radio show that was later renamed the *Melvin Purvis Law and Order Patrol*—Hoover insisted that Purvis be identified as a *former* FBI agent. And when Purvis died in 1960, Hoover (on the advice of his assistants) sent no letter of condolence to the former special agent's family.

Purvis died on February 29, 1960, at the age of fifty-six. Using the .38 Police Special he had carried on the night of the Dillinger shooting, he shot himself. Purvis's wife later sent a telegram to Hoover. It read: "We are honored that you ignored Melvin's death. Your jealousy hurt him very much but until the end I think he loved you."

fireman third class on the battleship U.S.S. *Utah*. Military life apparently did not agree with him. He was punished several times for being absent without leave (AWOL). In December 1923—less than five months after he enlisted—Dillinger left the navy for good. After he abandoned ship outside of Boston, he was labeled a deserter. The navy posted a $50 reward for the capture of Dillinger. It would not be the last reward posted for his capture.

By the spring of 1924, Dillinger had married a sixteen-year-old girl from Indiana named Beryl Ethel Hovius. The following autumn, he fell into serious trouble with the law. On September 6, 1924, Dillinger and Edgar Singleton robbed a sixty-five-year-old grocer named Frank Morgan. During the robbery, Morgan was struck on the head and a shot was accidentally fired.

The two robbers were soon caught. Dillinger pleaded guilty to two charges—conspiracy to commit a felony (a serious crime) and assault with intent to rob—having been assured by the prosecuting attorney that he would receive a light sentence. Dillinger's sentence was anything but light. Judge Joseph W. Williams made an example of the twenty-year-old robber by sentencing him to ten to twenty years in prison. Singleton, meanwhile, was tried before another judge. He received a lighter sentence and was paroled in less than two years.

AN EAGER STUDENT

When he entered the Indiana State Reformatory at Pendleton, Dillinger reportedly informed the warden that he would cause no trouble—except to escape. He made good on his word. Dillinger tried repeatedly to escape from Pendleton, and failed every time. While in prison he met a number of bank robbers, including Harry Pierpont and Homer Van Meter, both of whom were eventually sent to the state prison at Michigan City to serve out the remainder of their terms.

When Dillinger's parole hearing was held in 1929 (the year his wife divorced him), he was not released. But the parole board did listen to his plea to be sent to the Michigan City prison—supposedly to play on the prison's superior baseball team. In truth, Dillinger requested the transfer in order to rejoin Pierpont, who had much to teach him about the art of robbing banks.

Dillinger was transferred to the Michigan City prison on July 15, 1929. There he met several of Pierpont's associates, including Russell Lee Clark, John Hamilton, and Charles "Fat

Charley" Makley. When Dillinger was released on May 22, 1933—thanks, in part, to a petition signed by friends and neighbors—he left with a list of banks that were prime targets for robbery. Shortly after his release, Dillinger set about robbing the banks on Pierpont's list. But he did not rob the banks for personal gain. He was attempting to raise enough money to engineer the escape of Pierpont and some of his bank-robbing associates.

"X" MARKS THE SPOT

Over the course of three weeks, Dillinger robbed around ten banks in five mid-eastern states. Sometimes he worked alone, sometimes with others. But he was always well-dressed, and his *modus operandi*—or method of operation—rarely varied. An agile and athletic man, he was known for his ability to jump to the other side of a bank counter in a single bound.

The Pierpont Gang?

Dillinger worked with an assorted group of bank robbers known as the Dillinger Gang. But Dillinger was probably one of the least experienced bank robbers in the gang. Harry Pierpont, whom he had met in prison, was far more experienced and probably played a role in the leadership of the gang. Dillinger did not start pulling heists until after he had spent several years in jail, where he met a number of veteran bank robbers. The mob was reportedly dubbed the Dillinger Gang by a law official named Matt Leach—who wanted to create tension between Dillinger and Pierpont. The plan failed.

Once Dillinger had gathered enough money to organize the escape of his prison buddies, he traveled to Chicago. With some of the stolen funds, he bribed a foreman at a thread-making company to hide guns in a thread barrel that was to be delivered to the shirt-making shop at the Michigan City prison. The barrel was marked with a red "X" so that Pierpont would know where to look for the guns. On September 26, 1933, using the smuggled guns, ten prisoners escaped from the Michigan City penitentiary. The escapees, led by Pierpont, included Joseph Burns, Jim "Oklahoma Jack" Clark, Russell Clark, Walter Dietrich, Joseph Fox, John Hamilton, James Jenkins, Charles Makley, and Edward Shouse.

THE FIRST DILLINGER MOB

Dillinger was not able to celebrate his friends' new-found freedom. As Pierpont and the nine other inmates broke out of the Indiana institution, Dillinger—who had been captured at a

The Dillinger Squad

Intent on capturing the infamous bank robber, Chicago police assembled a "Dillinger Squad." The team consisted of forty officers who were permanently assigned to tracking the man known as "Gentleman Johnnie."

girlfriend's address in Dayton, Ohio—was in jail waiting to be charged for the robbery of the Bluffton Bank. But not for long. On October 12, Pierpont, Clark, and Makley returned Dillinger's favor. They broke into the Lima Jail where the bank robber was being held, fatally shot the sheriff, and escorted Dillinger to freedom.

Pierpont and Dillinger joined forces to create the first Dillinger mob. Using Chicago as their base of operations, they robbed between ten and twenty banks. Their method was nearly flawless. Walter Dietrich, one of the members of the Dillinger mob, had once belonged to a gang led by master bank robber Herman K. Lamm. The veteran bank robber shared Lamm's successful formula with the Dillinger gangsters in exchange for being allowed to participate in the Michigan City jail break. Lamm's method stressed careful planning and timing.

A SURE-FIRE METHOD

The Dillinger Gang based their bank-robbing method on the Lamm formula. They cased banks beforehand in order to find out where the money was kept, where guards were positioned, and where the alarm button was hidden. The gangsters reportedly made up some unusual cover stories in order to gain access to the bank. For instance, one of the mobsters supposedly posed as a movie director who was scouting out locations for a film shoot. After casing the bank, the gangsters drew up floor plans of the institution.

Time was an important factor. The gangsters calculated how much time they needed to relieve the bank of its money— and how much time they could operate without police interference. Like Lamm, Dillinger's gang used a stopwatch during a robbery. Normally, one of the gangsters was charged with keeping his eye on the stopwatch, calling out to the others when their time was up. The heist was abandoned—no matter how much money was left in the bank—after a certain amount of time had passed. Dillinger reportedly boasted that he could clear a bank out of money in less than five minutes.

The house in Tucson, Arizona, where John Dillinger was captured in January 1934. Three officers who participated in the capture stand in front of the house.

The gang's getaway was also planned out precisely. Street lights were timed. Backroads and alternate routes were noted in the plans. Often, the Dillinger gangsters did not race out of town on well-paved roads. Rather, they casually motored through a series of little-used back roads at a very modest speed.

THE WOODEN GUN INCIDENT

In January 1934, the first Dillinger Gang fell apart. Taking a break from robbery, the mobsters traveled to Florida and then to Tucson, Arizona. There, several members were arrested by police. Dillinger was extradited (sent to trial) to Indiana—or, as he claimed, "kidnapped" by a squad of Chicago detectives. The gangster was flown to Chicago and then escorted to the Crown

The hunt for Dillinger was, at that time, the largest manhunt in the history of the country. Newspapers kept track of the FBI's moves so that the public could follow the manhunt for the infamous bank robber. In fact, there was so much public interest in the manhunt that *Time* magazine printed a "Dillinger Land" map of the manhunt to be used as a party game.

Point Prison in Indiana, which enjoyed a reputation as an "escape-proof" jail.

Dillinger was held on a charge of shooting a policeman named William O'Malley during a bank robbery in East Chicago. He claimed that he was innocent (the charge was never proven). Choosing not to wait to go to trial, he broke out of jail. According to the newspapers of the day, Dillinger used a "wooden gun" to escape. After carving a gun out of the top of a wooden washboard, he colored it black with shoe polish. A later investigation carried out by the Hargrave Secret Service in Chicago provided another version of Dillinger's escape. According to the investigation, a well-bribed judge agreed to smuggle a real gun into the prison.

Whether the gun was fake or not, prison guards thought it was genuine. Dillinger captured several guards at gunpoint, locked them up, and took hold of two machine guns. He escaped with Herbert Youngblood, a thirty-five-year-old prisoner who was awaiting trial for murder, and two hostages, Deputy Sheriff Ernest Blunk and a mechanic named Ed Saager. Once they were safely away from the prison, Dillinger released the hostages—and gave them $4 for their trouble.

Lots of trouble at the Little Bohemia

Youngblood and Dillinger separated after their escape from Crown Point. Less than two weeks later—on March 16, 1934—Youngblood was killed by police in Port Huron, Michigan. Dillinger, meanwhile, assembled a second mob of bank robbers. The group, which is considered to be the "real" Dillinger Gang, included veteran bank robber Homer Van Meter and two of his associates, Tommy Carroll and Eddie Green. Also in the new gang were John Hamilton and a young man who had worked in the Chicago gangs of **Al Capone** (see entry) and **Bugs Moran** (see entry). The man was Lester Gillis—better known as Baby Face Nelson. An experienced bank robber and bootlegger, Nelson had a short temper and violent disposition.

Beginning on March 6, 1934—just three days after Dillinger's escape—the new gang set off on a bank robbing spree. Dillinger, who had driven across state lines in a stolen vehicle, was now hunted by federal officials. The Federal Bureau of Investigation (FBI) mounted what would become the largest manhunt in American history. Acting on a tip, FBI agents surrounded the Little Bohemia Lodge in the woods fifty miles outside of Rhinelander, Wisconsin. Inside the deserted vacation lodge was the bank robber's gang. It looked like Dillinger's time had come.

Barking dogs warned the gangsters of the intruders. Dillinger and the other gang members escaped. Unaware that the gangsters had fled, FBI agents continued their stakeout. When three men stepped out of the lodge and into a car, agents called out to the men—and then fired. Two of the men were wounded and the third, Eugene Boiseneau, was killed. All three were innocent bystanders.

The federal bureau of unpopular investigations

Following Dillinger's death, FBI press releases announced that the gangster had been shot after he resisted arrest and attempted to draw a pistol. FBI director J. Edgar Hoover later wrote in his memoirs, *Persons in Hiding,* that "living true to his real character of a sneak and a coward, [Dillinger] had attempted to throw a woman in front of him to act as a barricade as he attempted to draw his gun."

But witnesses did not support the FBI's story. Not for the first time, the public was outraged by the FBI's handling of the Dillinger manhunt. A Virginia newspaper echoed this sentiment: "Any brave man would have walked down the aisle [of the movie theater] and arrested Dillinger. . . . Why were there so many cowards afraid of this one man? The answer is that the federal agents are, for the most part, cowards."

ENEMIES IN THE BUREAU

The public was outraged by the FBI's inability to capture Dillinger, and by the agency's failure to protect law-abiding citizens. In particular, bureau director J. Edgar Hoover and agent Melvin Purvis, who was responsible for the Little Bohemia disaster, received harsh criticism for their role in the Dillinger manhunt. Dillinger was making a mockery of the bureau. Hoover increased the reward offered for the bank robber's capture—and issued an order for his agents to shoot to kill.

In July 1934, Chicago police informed federal agents that Dillinger's whereabouts had been established. And a friend—a Romanian immigrant named Anna Sage—had agreed to betray him. In exchange, Sage wanted the reward money and assurance that immigration authorities would not follow through on her deportation (expulsion from the country). Melvin Purvis received word that on the evening of July 22, 1934, Sage and a waitress named Polly Hamilton would attend a movie at the Biograph Theater on the North Side of Chicago—accompanied by the fugitive bank robber.

A NIGHT AT THE MOVIES

The government agents were not sure that they would be able to identify Dillinger. Although his photograph had been printed in newspapers, wanted posters, and detective magazines throughout the country, he had recently undergone plastic surgery to alter his appearance. Sage (later known as "the Lady in Red") wore a red dress to make sure that she could be easily identified. Agents watched as Dillinger and the women entered the theater. At Hoover's command, they waited until the movie was over to make their move.

Inside, Dillinger watched *Manhattan Melodrama*—the story of the rise and fall of a good-looking and likable gambler, played by Clark Gable. The movie ends as Gable heads for the electric chair. At about 10:40 P.M., Dillinger left the theater with his companions. He was wearing his customary straw hat and dark glasses. Three men followed them closely. Suddenly, the women stepped away from Dillinger, and federal agents fired. The gangster was shot dead in an alley next to the theater. (A woman bystander was wounded as well.)

Immediately after the shooting, bystanders collected souvenirs of Dillinger's death—even dipping their handkerchiefs in the dead gangster's blood. Two days later, on July 24, Dillinger's body was buried in the outskirts of Indianapolis. Five thousand people attended the funeral ceremony. In order to prevent souvenir-hunters from disturbing the grave, Dillinger's father had it covered with reinforced concrete.

THE END OF THE SECOND DILLINGER GANG

For a while, Nelson took over Dillinger's role as "Public Enemy Number One." He died the following November from wounds he received in a gun battle with FBI agents. Van Meter was killed after he, too, was betrayed by friends. Green died at the hands of FBI gunmen. Less than five months after Dillinger's death, the second Dillinger Gang was destroyed.

Pierpont and Makley were sentenced to death for the murder of a sheriff in 1931. Using guns carved from soap, they fought their way out of Ohio State Prison in Columbus. Ambushed by a riot squad, Pierpont was wounded and Makley was killed. Pierpont was executed the following month.

Purvis was unable to intervene in Sage's deportation proceedings. The infamous "Lady in Red" was deported to Europe. She died in 1947.

Take a look at this!

Dillinger (1991) stars Mark Harmon as the Depression-era bank robber, who became Public Enemy Number One. Sherilyn Fenn plays girlfriend Billy Frenchette, with Will Patton as G-man Purvis.

Sources for Further Reading

Bruns, Roger. *The Bandit Kings from Jesse James to Pretty Boy Floyd.* New York: Crown, 1995, pp. 176–210.

Dartford, Mark, ed. *Crimes and Punishment,* Volume 6. Tarrytown, NY: Marshall Canvendish, 1985, pp. 866–877.

Nash, Jay Robert. *Bloodletters and Badmen.* New York: M. Evans, 1973, pp. 159–178.

Nash, Jay Robert. *The Encyclopedia of World Crime.* Wilmette, IL: Crime Books, 1990, pp. 2513–2514.

Prassel, Frank Richard. *The Great American Outlaw, A Legacy of Fact and Fiction.* Norman: University of Oklahoma Press, 1993, pp. 277–283.

Sifakis, Carl. *The Encyclopedia of American Crime.* New York: Facts on File, 1982, pp. 206–210, 596–597.

Vandome, Nick. *Crimes and Criminals.* New York: Chambers, 1992, pp. 80–81.

Belle Gunness

Born: 1859
Died: ?

A middle-aged widow who lured men to her home with promises of marriage, Belle Gunness made a business out of murder—and then disappeared.

THE WIDOW SORENSON

Born in Norway, Gunness moved to the United States at the age of twenty-four. Her family background is sketchy. Her father may have been a stonemason (a builder who works with stones) or a traveling magician. She probably had a sister who also moved to America. In 1884, shortly after she left Norway, Gunness married Mads Albert Sorenson in Chicago. Gunness and Sorenson had three children—Jennie, Myrtle, and Lucy (one or all of whom had been adopted).

In 1900, Mads Sorenson died. Although Gunness claimed her husband died of heart failure, his family suspected foul play. Adding to their suspicion was the fact that Gunness had tried to collect on her husband's $8,500 life insurance policy—just one day after the funeral. Although the family is believed to have ordered an inquest (inquiry), there is no evidence that the coroner pursued the case. Gunness collected a handsome sum from her husband's insurance policy.

"Come prepared to stay forever"

Belle Gunness lured men to her farm in La Porte, Indiana, by placing personal ads in newspapers. When a suitable candidate responded, she began corresponding with him, eventually inviting him to her home. Andrew Hegelein was among the men Gunness wrote to. In a letter dated January 13, 1908, she wrote:

To the Dearest Friend in the World: No woman in the world is happier than I am. I know that you are now to come to me and be my own. I can tell from your letters that you are the man I want. It does not take one long to tell when to like a person, and you I like better than anyone in the world, I know.

Think how we will enjoy each other's company. You, the sweetest man in the whole world. We will be all alone with each other. Can you conceive of anything nicer? I think of you constantly. When I hear your name mentioned, and this is when one of the dear children speaks of you, or I hear myself humming it with the words of an old love song, it is beautiful music to my ears.

My heart beats in wild rapture for you, My Andrew, I love you. Come prepared to stay forever.

Andrew Hegelein never returned from his trip to La Porte. In May of 1908, his remains were found buried on the grounds of the Gunness farm.

In 1902, at the age of forty-two, Gunness appeared in La Porte, Indiana. She purchased a farm near town and soon married a local man, Peter Gunness, who was also a native of Norway. Shortly after their son, Philip, was born in 1903, Peter died. According to Gunness's story, Peter—who was a butcher—had been killed when a heavy instrument fell from a shelf, splitting his skull. Again, Gunness's story was questioned and again there was no evidence to indicate that she was a murderer. Gunness pocketed another $4,000 in insurance money, in spite of the local coroner's insistence that Peter's "accident" had been planned.

OBJECT: MATRIMONY

Gunness's fourteen-year-old daughter, Jennie, reportedly told people that her mother had killed her father with a meat cleaver—although she denied saying so when the coroner questioned her. Two years after Peter's death, in September 1906, Jennie disappeared. Gunness told neighbors that she had sent

A bad poem about a bad woman

Gunness's exploits were described by an anonymous poet whose rhymes were sometimes far-fetched:

Belle Gunness lived in In-di-an;
She always, always had a man;
Ten, at least, went in her door—
And were never, never seen no more.
Now, all these men were Norska [Scandinavian] folk
Who came to Belle from Minn-e-sote;
They liked their coffee and their gin:
They got it—plus a mickey finn [a drugged drink].
And now with cleaver poised so sure
Belle neatly cut their jug-u-lar [a vein in the neck]
She put them in a bath of lime
And left them there for quite some time.
There's red upon the Hoosier [Indiana] moon
For Belle was strong and full of doom;
And think of all them Norska men
Who'll never see St. Paul again.

the girl to a boarding school in Los Angeles, California.

Gunness continued to raise and butcher hogs using the skills she had probably learned from her second husband. She hired a Canadian farmhand named Ray Lamphere (or L'Amphere) to help her run the farm, and by the end of 1906 had begun to place matrimonial (marriage-related) personal ads in newspapers in Chicago and other cities in the Midwest. She also placed some ads in Norwegian-language papers. In her ads, Gunness claimed to be a young, attractive, well-to-do widow who was looking for a financially secure man to marry: "Rich, goodlooking widow, young, owner of a large farm, wishes to get in touch with a gentleman of wealth with cultured tastes. Object, matrimony. No triflers need apply." She also added that her prospective suitor had to be willing to pay off the $1,000 mortgage on her farm.

John Moo (or Moe), a Wisconsinite, was one of the first to reply. A middle-aged Norwegian native, he arrived in La Porte with more than $1,000—and vanished within days of his arrival. Other marriage-minded men followed. Ole Budsburg, a widower from Wisconsin, and Andrew Hegelein, a single farmer from South Dakota, were among the men who traveled to the Gunness farm and were never heard from again.

On April 6, 1907, Budsburg left the La Porte Savings Bank with thousands of dollars in cash. It was the last time he was seen alive. When his sons, Matthew and Oscar, wrote to Gunness to ask about their father, she replied that she had never

seen the man. Similarly, Hegelein disappeared in January 1908, shortly after he was seen with Gunness depositing a $2,900 check at the Savings Bank.

The Gunness farm, where many dead bodies were found. The letters A through E indicate individual graves--each hole contained from one to four bodies.

A TIMELY FIRE

On February 3, 1908, Gunness fired Ray Lamphere, who was reportedly in love with her. She hired Joe Maxon in his place. Asle Hegelein, meanwhile, had become concerned about his brother's failure to return home. He wrote to Gunness, who informed him that Andrew was not on her farm—although she would be willing, for a price, to help look for him.

No doubt Gunness was concerned about mounting questions and loose ends. Pesky relatives, nosey neighbors, and a

False teeth

Gunness wore dentures—a porcelain plate of false teeth that was anchored to a tooth in her mouth. Although the plate was found among the ruins, it did not help investigators identify the body: Gunness could have left the dentures, possibly pulling out one of her teeth, to create a false impression that she had died in the fire.

disgruntled former employee who knew too much about her matrimonial scam. Gunness approached a lawyer named M. E. Leliter to ask him to draw up a will. She claimed that she was afraid for her life because Lamphere, she said, had threatened to set her farmhouse on fire. Gunness paid off the mortgage on her house and drew up a will that left everything to her children. But she didn't inform the police that Lamphere had threatened her life.

On April 28, 1908, Gunness's farmhouse burned to the ground. Joe Maxon, the handyman, escaped by jumping from the second floor. Gunness and her three children died in the fire—or so it seemed. Four bodies were found in the basement, beneath the rubble of the collapsed house. Three of the corpses were those of children, and the fourth was the badly burned body of a woman—a decapitated (beheaded) woman. Without a head, the corpse (body) could not be positively identified as the body of Gunness.

A PIGSTY FULL OF BONES

A number of things led people to question whether Belle Gunness had died in the fire. Two farmers viewed the body and stated that it couldn't possibly have been the remains of their neighbor. A number of Gunness's friends, some of whom had come from Chicago, agreed. What's more, Gunness was a tall woman who weighed about 200 pounds. The corpse was that of a woman who stood five feet, three inches tall—five inches shorter than Gunness—and weighed under one hundred and fifty pounds. Physicians compared measurements taken from the corpse with those taken by tailors who made Gunness's clothing. Their findings were clear: the headless body was not the corpse of Belle Gunness. The body was then examined by Dr. J. Meyers, who determined that the unknown woman had died of strychnine poisoning.

On May 3, 1908, Sheriff Albert H. Smutzer sent a crew of men to Gunness's farm. Digging around the area where the hogs were fed, they uncovered a grisly patchwork of shallow

Lucrative crime spree

In a murder spree that lasted from 1901 to 1908, Gunness collected somewhere between $100,000 and $250,000 from her victims.

graves. They found the body of Gunness's daughter, Jennie, as well as the corpses of two other unidentified children. The remains of Moo, Budsburg, and Hegelein were also uncovered. By the end of the search, the bodies of at least fourteen men had been discovered. And not all in one piece: an expert butcher, Gunness had cut up many of the bodies.

Ray Lamphere was arrested and charged with murder and arson. Although he admitted to setting the fire, he pleaded innocent to the charges of murder. Tried on May 22, 1908, he was acquitted of murder. He was, however, convicted of arson, and was sentenced to up to twenty years in prison. Lamphere died after less than two years in prison, but not before he confessed to Reverend E. A. Schell.

FIFTY WAYS TO LOSE YOUR LOVER

Lamphere outlined the gruesome details of his service as Gunness's employee. Although he continued to deny killing anyone, he confessed to helping Gunness bury the bodies of a number of men. He also described Gunness's methods. Sometimes she drugged her victim's coffee, waited for him to lose consciousness, and split his head with a cleaver (large butcher knife). Others she simply poisoned with strychnine. Some bodies she buried intact, and others she dissected. She also threw victims' corpses into a vat of hot water (which was used to scald slaughtered hogs) and then covered them with quicklime (substance that burns, like acid). Lamphere claimed that Gunness had taken thousands of dollars from her victims, some of whom had come the farm with their life savings.

Lamphere also claimed to know about the bodies in the basement. The woman, he said, had been hired as a housekeeper—only to serve as Gunness's stand-in during the blaze. Gunness dressed the woman in her clothes, dragged her to the basement, and left her own false teeth behind. The three other corpses belonged to Gunness's children. Prior to the fire, she had knocked them unconscious using chloroform (liquid anesthetic). She then suffocated them and placed them in the basement next to the headless woman.

Lamphere claimed that he was supposed to meet Gunness after the fire. He never saw her again and died in jail on December 30, 1909.

No teeth, no name
A headless woman was found in the ashes of the Gunness farmhouse. This made identification impossible: the head would have contained teeth and dental work that could have been traced.

Sources for Further Reading

Nash, Jay Robert. *Bloodletters and Badmen.* New York: M. Evans, 1973, pp. 252, 382–387.

Nash, Jay Robert. *The Encyclopedia of World Crime.* Wilmette, IL: Crime Books, 1990, pp. 1400–1405.

Nash, Jay Robert. *Look for the Woman, A Narrative Encyclopedia of Female Poisoners, Kidnappers, Thieves, Extortionists, Terrorists, Swindlers, and Spies, from Elizabethan Times to the Present.* New York: M. Evans, 1981, pp. 176–178.

Vandome, Nick. *Crimes and Criminals.* New York: Chambers, 1992, p. 102.

Pearl Hart

Born: 1871
Died: 1925?
AKA: Mrs. L. P. Keele

Had Pearl Hart pulled a stagecoach robbery thirty years earlier, she probably would not have earned a spot in the history books. But because she and her accomplice botched a robbery in 1899—at the end of the stagecoach era—she staked her claim to fame as the perpetrator of the last American stagecoach robbery.

MARRIED LIFE AND OLD WEST SHOWS

Pearl Taylor was born into to a well respected middle-class family in Lindsay, Ontario, Canada. One of several children, she was educated at an all-girl boarding school in Toronto. At the age of seventeen she eloped (ran away to marry) with Frederick Hart—a man who liked to gamble and had no steady job.

In 1893 the Harts attended the Columbian Exposition in Chicago, Illinois—a large fair with many sideshows. For some time Frederick worked at the Columbian Exposition while Pearl worked various jobs. Pearl was captivated by the Wild West shows—exciting dramatizations of life on the frontier—and she reportedly learned to ride a horse and shoot a gun from some of the show's performers. When the Exposition ended Pearl left her husband and headed West, to Trinidad, Colorado. There she worked briefly as a hotel maid and gave birth to a son. Returning to Lindsay, she left the boy with her mother and set off to Phoenix, Arizona. Pearl worked as a cook and took in laundry to support herself.

A long stagecoach ride was not to be taken lightly. In 1877 the *Omaha Herald* printed suggestions that applied to anyone who traveled by stage. Here are some of the newspaper's *Hints for Plains Travelers:*

The best seat inside a stage coach is the one next to the driver. You will have to ride with back to the horses, which with some people, produces an illness not unlike sea-sickness, but in a long journey this will wear off, and you will get more rest, with less than half the bumps and jars than on any other seat. When any old "sly Eph," [clever fellow] who traveled thousands of miles on coaches, offers through sympathy to exchange his back or middle seat with you, don't do it. Never ride in cold weather with tight boots or shoes, nor close-fitting gloves. Bathe your feet before starting in cold water, and wear loose overshoes and gloves two or three sizes too large. When the driver asks you to get off and walk, do it without grumbling. He will not request it unless absolutely necessary. If a team runs

In 1895, Frederick traveled to Phoenix hoping to get back together with his wife. The couple reconciled and Frederick took work as a hotel manager and bartender. But their second attempt to live together didn't last long. Within three years, after the birth of a daughter, Frederick left Pearl. According to one version, he left to join the army fighting the Spanish in Cuba. Another report claims that he left after Pearl shot at him. Whatever his reasons, Frederick left in 1898, and never returned.

The last Arizona stage

After leaving her second child with her mother, Hart returned to the West, working as a cook in mining camps. During this time, she met her future partner in crime, Joe Boot—a man who has been described in conflicting accounts as a miner, a town drunk, and a dashing British bandit. Historians are also unclear about who was responsible for setting the robbery in motion. Whether it was Boot's quick-fix scheme or Hart's plan to come up with money for her ailing mother, the two devised a plot to rob a local stage in 1899.

The stagecoach that traveled the sixty-five miles between Florence and Globe was the last of its kind in the Arizona Terri-

away, sit still and take your chances; if you jump nine times out of ten you will be hurt. . . . Don't smoke a strong pipe inside especially early in the morning, spit on the leeward side of the coach [the side of the coach the wind blows *away* from]. If you have anything to take in a bottle, pass it around; a man who drinks by himself in such a case is lost to all human feeling. . . . Be sure and take two heavy blankets with you; you will need them. Don't swear, nor lop [lean] over on your neighbor when sleeping. Don't ask how far it is to the next station until you get there. Take small change to pay expenses. Never attempt to fire a gun or pistol while on the road; it may frighten the team and the careless handling and cocking of the weapon makes nervous people nervous. Don't discuss politics or religion, nor point out places on the road where horrible murders have been committed, if delicate women are among the passengers. . . . Don't imagine for a moment you are going on a pic-nic; expect annoyance, discomfort and some hardships. If you are disappointed, thank heaven.

tory. The Globe stage hadn't been robbed for years—and with good reason. At the turn of the century, stagecoaches were an outdated form of transportation—and they no longer carried Wells Fargo strongboxes that had been the targets of earlier highway robbers. In fact, there was so little of value on board the stagecoaches of that era that most didn't even bother to carry a "shotgun rider" to protect the passengers and cargo.

Hart and Boot went ahead with the robbery anyway. Holding guns on the driver, Boot and Hart (who was dressed in pants and wore her hair short) took the driver's gun and relieved the passengers of the contents of their wallets. With a little over $400 for their efforts, the two bandits sent the stage on its way—and promptly got lost. They had neglected to plan their escape. Within three days of the robbery, local lawmen found Hart and Boot asleep. According to one account, they were found within *one mile* of the spot where they had stopped the stagecoach.

THE LADY BANDIT

The robbery had been a miserable failure, but that didn't matter to Hart's contemporaries, who treated her like a star. Crowds of onlookers and autograph-seekers gathered at the Globe jail, where the "Lady Bandit" was held before her trial.

Tried separately from Boot, she was acquitted by a jury that was probably swayed by her hard-luck story. The judge was not pleased. After ordering her to be tried on a separate weapons charge, Judge Doan sentenced Hart to five years in the Yuma Territorial prison. Boot, meanwhile, was sentenced to a thirty-year stay at the same prison.

Hart served only a portion of her sentence. Some say she suddenly "got religion" and started preaching that crime doesn't pay. Others claim that Governor A. W. Brodie gave in to public pressure to release her. Still others suggest that she was quietly pardoned to cover-up an embarrassing—and difficult to explain—pregnancy. In any case, on December 19, 1902—after only eighteen months in prison—Hart left Yuma prison a free woman.

For the most part, Hart stayed out of the public eye after she was released except, possibly, for a brief stint in Buffalo Bill's Wild West Show. In Kansas City, Missouri—under the name of Mrs. L. P. Keele—she was arrested and jailed for a short time. The details of her death are uncertain: there is no way to verify whether she died in Kansas City when she was in her fifties, as some historians claim—or whether she lived into her nineties on a ranch in Globe, as other sources suggest.

Visiting the past

Hart reportedly returned to the Globe jailhouse in 1924 to survey her former lodging. When the guard asked who she was, she replied--so the story goes--"Pearl Hart, the lady bandit."

Sources for Further Reading

The American West, A Cultural Encyclopedia, Volumes 5 and 9, Danbury, CT: Grolier Educational Corp., 1995, pp. 756, 825, 1507-1511.

Collins, William and Bruce Levene. *Black Bart: The True Story of the West's Most Famous Stagecoach Robber.* Mendocino, CA: Pacific Transcriptions, 1992, pp. 24-39.

Davis, William C. *The American Frontier.* New York: Smithmark, 1992, pp. 32-33, 180.

Lewis, Jon. *The Mammoth Book of the West.* New York: Carroll & Graf, 1996, p. 335.

Metz, Leon Claire. *A Gallery of Notorious Gunmen from the American West: The Shooters.* New York: Berkeley Books, 1996, pp. 247–250.

Nash, Jay Robert. *Bloodletters and Badmen.* New York: M. Evans, 1973, pp. 61–62.

Ross, Stewart. *Fact or Fiction: Cowboys.* Surrey, British Columbia: Copper Beech, 1995, p. 31.

The Wild West. [Online] Available http://www.calweb.com/~rbbusman/women/hart.htm, February 7, 1997.

The bandit actress

After Hart was released from prison, she starred—very briefly—in a play called *The Arizona Bandit.* She was a natural in the role: the play, written by her sister, was about her life as an outlaw.

Patty Hearst

Born: February 20, 1954
AKA: Tania

Kidnapped as a young woman, Patty Hearst was transformed into "Tania" during her nineteen-month odyssey as a captive—and then a member—of the Symbionese Liberation Army. A participant in a number of robberies, she later claimed to have been brainwashed. Although convicted and imprisoned, she eventually received a pardon.

THE HEARST LEGACY

The middle child of five daughters, Hearst was born in San Francisco, California, on February 20, 1954. Her father, Randolph Apperson Hearst, was chairman of the board of the Hearst Corporation—the largest privately owned media conglomerate (a business coporation made up of a number of companies) in the United States. Hearst's mother, Catherine Wood (Campbell) Hearst, was a member of the governing board of the University of California. Her position earned her a reputation as an outspoken conservative. Hearst's legendary grandfather, William Randolph Hearst Jr., amassed a fortune as the founder of the Hearst newspaper empire.

Hearst grew up on family estates in Beverly Hills and Hillsborough, California. She spent vacations at family ranches, such as Wyntoon and San Simeon. A one-hundred-and-forty acre estate, San Simeon is the largest single piece of privately owned land on the Pacific Coast. The grounds include an enormous castle that was commissioned by Hearst's eccentric grandfather.

In an autobiography published in 1982, Hearst recalled that her family's wealth helped her develop self-assurance: "I grew up in this affluent [wealthy] and sheltered environment sublimely self-confident," she wrote. "But we were never spoiled. . . . What I remember most keenly about those years was my parents' strictness."

CATHOLIC SCHOOL AND BERKELEY

Hearst attended Catholic boarding schools as a girl. She graduated from the Convent of the Sacred Heart in Menlo Park, California, and then began high school at Santa Catalina School in Montery, California. While she excelled in English and History, she received average grades in subjects she did not enjoy, such as French and Math. As a junior, she transferred to an exclusive day school in Hillsborough, the Crystal Springs School for Girls. Hearst's grades improved at Crystal Springs, and she graduated in June 1971, one year ahead of the rest of her classmates.

While at Crystal Springs, Hearst was tutored by Steven Weed, a young teacher at the school. The two eventually moved in together and eventually became engaged. During Hearst's first year at Menlo College, she lived with Weed in an apartment two miles from campus. She earned all As and was named the school's best student of the year. After spending the summer in Europe, Hearst moved to Berkeley, California, where Weed had been awarded a teaching grant to pursue his graduate studies. Hearst enrolled in the University of California for the winter and spring terms of 1972 to 1973. Majoring in veterinary science (the treatment of animals), she took courses in chemistry, math, and zoology. Again, her grades were average. The following school year she changed her major to art history, and immediately began to earn high marks.

KIDNAPPED BY THE SLA

At 9:20 P.M. on February 4, 1974—two months after Hearst and Weed had announced their engagement—two men and one

The high cost of living

The kidnapping of Patricia Hearst—and its aftermath—cost the Hearst family a fortune. Randolph Hearst spent at least $2 million trying to get his daughter ransomed—in the form of a food program to feed poor people in California. After Patty's capture, Randolph posted $1.5 million in bail—of which he paid $100,000 in cash. Fearing for his daughter's life during the trial, he hired bodyguards to watch her around the clock—for a fee that is estimated at $200,000 (plus a very expensive guard dog). Legal fees and expenses added more than $1 million more to the tab.

A failure to communicate

When police captured SLA members Russell Little and Joseph Romero, following the slaying of Oakland school superintendent Marcus Foster, they found a "hit list" among their belongings. The SLA's hit list named Patty Hearst, the daughter of one of the nation's wealthiest families, as a potential future victim. The police never informed her.

woman broke into their apartment on Benvenue Street. Weed was beaten and knocked unconscious with a wine bottle. Hearst, who was screaming and partially clothed, was abducted at gunpoint.

Hearst's kidnappers were members of the Symbionese Liberation Army (SLA), a left-wing terrorist group. (Left-wing terrorist groups pursue political goals by extreme, revolutionary, and sometimes violent means.) Founded in Berkeley, the group was headed by Donald Defreeze, an African American petty criminal who had escaped from Soledad prison in 1972. Appointing himself "general field marshal" in the army, Defreeze called himself Cinque Mtume, a Swahili name meaning "Fifth Prophet." Defreeze originally recruited nine members to his radical organization, including Russell Little (known as Bo) and Joseph Romero (known as Osceola). The SLA first captured public attention on November 6, 1973, after members murdered Marcus Foster, the first African American superintendent of schools in Oakland, California. Little and Romero, the only gang members captured in the slaying, were sentenced to serve terms at San Quentin penitentiary outside San Francisco, California.

Originally, SLA members planned to organize a hostage exchange in which they would trade their "prisoner of war," Hearst, for Little and Romero. But the kidnapping generated so much publicity that they decided to change their plan. They decided to hold on to their hostage indefinitely.

BRAINWASHING, BANK ROBBERY, AND DISNEYLAND

First, Hearst was subjected to fifty-seven days of confinement. Bound and blindfolded in a closet, she was also raped and psychologically tortured. Hearst later claimed that her kidnappers used control and abuse to brainwash her. (Brainwashing involves replacing an individual's beliefs with opposing beliefs.)

Opposite page: Patty Hearst in front of the Symbionese Liberation Army symbol, brandishing an automatic weapon.

An artist turned terrorist

Wendy Misako Yoshimura was born in a California detention camp, where Japanese Americans were forcefully detained during World War II (1939-1945). The daughter of gardeners, she was a prize-winning artist who turned to terrorism in the early 1970s.

In March 1972, a police raid uncovered a stash of bombs, explosives, rifles, and shotguns in a garage that Yoshimura had rented under the name of Annie Wong. Formally charged with illegal possession of weapons in connection with a plot to blow up a Navy Reserve Officers Training Corps building on the University of California campus, she pleaded guilty—and disappeared. Her former boyfriend, William Brandt, was imprisoned at Soledad prison on the same charges. Yoshimura managed to avoid capture for more than three years. During that period she joined with SLA members—sometime after the Los Angeles shootout. Yoshimura's odyssey ended on September 18, 1975, when FBI agents and police arrested the Japanese American terrorist along with Hearst. During her trial and sentencing, Hearst informed on many of her former underground associates—including Yoshimura, a woman she reportedly once adored.

On April 5, 1974, she recorded a message to announce publicly that she had joined the SLA. Claiming to have joined the organization of her own free will, she took the name of "Tania."

Ten days later members of the SLA robbed the Hibernia Bank's Sunset District branch in San Francisco, California. Hearst was among the robbers. Later that day, the evening news carried surveillance footage that showed Hearst wearing a beret and carrying a rifle. William Saxbe, the U.S. attorney general, publicly labeled her a "common criminal." Once considered a victim, Hearst had become a villain in public opinion.

Pursued by the police, the SLA moved from San Francisco to the Compton ghetto in Los Angeles, California. Hearst next surfaced on May 16, 1974, when she and two other SLA members—William and Emily Harris—stopped at Mel's Sporting Goods on Crenshaw Boulevard. After security guards began to wrestle with William Harris, who had been accused of attempting to shoplift a pair of socks, Hearst fired an automatic rifle at the store from a van parked outside. The trio fled in the van and then quickly abandoned it. Using other vehicles, they drove thirty miles south of Los Angeles, to Anaheim, where they rented a motel room at Disneyland.

MORE VIOLENCE

The abandoned van contained something the bank robbers had overlooked: a parking ticket. The ticket lead police right to the SLA's doorstep. Moving from their safehouse to a home on East 54th Street, SLA members engaged in a violent shootout with police. After the house was demolished by fire, the remains of Defreeze and five other SLA members were found among the ashes.

Hearst and the Harrises watched the shootout on the television in their room in Anaheim. Within a few days, the three surviving SLA members issued a taped statement. Reading a script written by Emily Harris, Hearst denounced (rejected) her parents, whom she called "the pig Hearsts." She also professed love for William Wolfe, an SLA member who had died in the shootout.

The three criminals avoided capture by hiding in various safe spots across the country. Aided by outsiders who were sympathetic to their cause, they hid in a farmhouse in South Canaan, Pennsylvania, in the early summer of 1974. In July, they moved to a farm in Jeffersonville, New York, returning to California at the end of the summer.

In Sacramento, the group gathered a small number of new recruits, including a brother and sister, Kathleen and Steven Soliah. In February 1975, the new group robbed the Guild Savings and Loan Association near Sacramento, and in April they hit the Crocker National Bank in the Sacramento area. A bank customer died in the Crocker robbery, after having been shot by Emily Harris. Hearst drove the getaway vehicle. Returning to San Francisco, the group bombed a number of police cars—both in the San Francisco area and in Los Angeles.

A MASSIVE MANHUNT

Meanwhile, SLA members were tracked by a manhunt that involved more than three thousand Federal Bureau of Investigation (FBI) agents who interviewed, followed, or background-checked almost thirty thousand individuals from coast to coast.

Lights, camera, action!

With her kidnapping and trial behind her, Hearst tried her hand at acting. The one-time terrorist appeared in *Serial Mom* (1994)—in which she plays "juror number eight," who is beaten to death by the serial mom herself, Kathleen Turner. Hearst also appeared in *Cry Baby* (1990)—as Traci Lords's crossing-guard mom—and supplied a radio call-in voice for a 1997 episode of the television show, *Frasier.*

Citizen Hearst

Patty Hearst's grandfather, William Randolph Hearst Jr., earned a fortune as a newspaper publisher. Sixteen years after his death, *Forbes* magazine estimated the total worth of his estate to be well over the $500 million mark and quickly approaching $1 billion. Hearst provided the role model for the character of Charles Foster Kane in the Orson Welles film, *Citizen Kane*—generally considered to be one of the finest movies ever made.

The investigation also involved local police from Alaska to New York—and even Hong Kong. After receiving a tip, the FBI located the two-story farm house in Pennsylvania where Hearst and the Harrises had hidden. Police dogs picked up Hearst's scent in one of the beds. After dusting rooms for evidence, agents found fingerprints belonging to William and Emily Harris as well as those of another person—Wendy Yoshimura, a Japanese American woman who was wanted in a Berkeley, California, bombing conspiracy.

With a new lead to pursue, the FBI began to look into Yoshimura's background. After learning that Yoshimura's former boyfriend, William Brandt, was imprisoned at Soledad penitentiary, the FBI monitored the visitors he received. Kathleen Soliah was among Brandt's visitors.

Next agents began to check out Soliah—as well as her younger brother, Steven. Investigating the activities of the twenty-seven-year-old house painter, agents discovered that Steven Soliah had rented an apartment at 625 Morse Street. The investigation also led to another San Francisco address—288 Precita Street, a few miles away—into which a young couple had recently moved.

TIME RUNS OUT

FBI agents suspected that the Harrises were living at the Precita Street apartment. From surveillance vehicles parked on the street, they thought they saw William Harris leaving the apartment. In order to make a positive identification, one agent, dressed as a hippie, followed the man to a laundromat. Convinced that they had located the SLA fugitives, FBI agents had local police seal off the block surrounding the Precita Street apartment. Shortly after 1 P.M. on September 18, 1975, William and Emily jogged around the corner toward their apartment. They were arrested.

Less certain about who they would find at the other address, the FBI sent only two agents to investigate the apartment at 625 Morse. Arriving with two policemen, they ordered the occupants to open the door. At gunpoint, Wendy Yoshimura opened the apartment door. Agents caught another woman as she tried to escape. The woman—who weighed less than ninety pounds—was Hearst. A later search of the apartment turned up four pistols (in addition to two that were hidden in the women's purses), two sawed-off shotguns, and a marijuana plant.

URBAN GUERILLA

Hearst's arrest received tremendous publicity. Taken to the federal building in San Francisco in handcuffs, she smiled and lifted her clenched fist. Hearst's militant (combative) pose appeared nation-wide—and around the world—in newspapers and on television. On the jailhouse booking form she listed "Urban Guerrilla" (terrorist) as her occupation. But Hearst's jailhouse swagger did not last long. She later told a reporter, "The more I talked to psychiatrists, I just started breaking down. I started realizing that I was terribly confused."

On May 9, 1977, Hearst was sentenced to five years' probation on state charges involving the incident at the sporting goods store. (A convict who is sentenced to probation is given a trial period in which he or she is expected to abide by the law.) But the federal charges—armed robbery and the use of a firearm—were much more serious. In spite of all the money and resources at the Hearst family's disposal, she was found guilty on both counts. On April 12, 1976, she was temporarily sentenced to twenty-five years for robbery and ten years for the use of a firearm—the maximum sentence for each offense. On September 24, she received her final sentence: two seven-year terms, to be served one after the other.

RELEASED FROM PRISON

The Hearst family did not give up easily. After the U.S. Supreme Court refused to hear the case, a national Committee for the Release of Patricia Hearst circulated a petition that was signed by forty-eight congressmen. In January of 1979, President Jimmy

Take a look at this!

Hearst's ordeal inspired nearly ten books and a number of movies, including *Patty Hearst* (1988), starring Natasha Richardson. Based on Hearst's autobiography, the film opens with the newspaper heiress's kidnapping and ends just before her prison sentence is commuted by President Jimmy Carter. Director Schrader called the film "a real journey, an emotional rollercoaster. It's the story of how a person survives, a tribute to the resiliency [ability to recover] of the individual."

Costly manhunt

The nineteen-month nation-wide manhunt for Patty Hearst cost taxpayers an estimated $5 million.

Randolph and Catherine Hearst, Patty's parents, plead with their daughter's abductors for her safe return.

Carter commuted (lessened) Hearst's sentence. On February 1, after serving only twenty-two months and seventeen days in prison, Hearst was released. Interviewed after her sentence was commuted, she wore a T-shirt bearing the words "Pardon Me."

On April 1, 1979, Hearst married Bernard Shaw, a policeman who worked as her bodyguard during the trial. (Her maid of honor was Trish Tobin, a childhood friend whose father owned the Hibernia Bank that Hearst and the SLA robbed.) The couple moved to New England with their two daughters.

Sources for Further Reading

Contemporary Authors Volume 136. Detroit: Gale Research, 1992, pp. 184-185.

Earl Blackwell's Celebrity Register 1990. Detroit: Gale Research, 1990, p. 195.

Fosburgh, Lacey. "Patty Today." *The New York Times Biographical Service* (April 1977), pp. 545–549.

Lovece, Frank. "Heiress Human." *Entertainment Weekly* (April 22, 1994), p. 37.

Matthews, Tom, et al. "The Story of Patty." *Newsweek* (September 29, 1975), pp. 20–40.

Nash, Jay Robert. *Look for the Woman: A Narrative Encyclopedia of Female Poisoners, Kidnappers, Thieves, Extortionists, Terrorists, Swindlers, and Spies, from Elizabethan Times to the Present.* New York: M. Evans, 1981, pp. 188–189.

Sinclair, Tom. "Patty Hearst Turns Symbionese: The Kidnapped Heiress' Ordeal Of Torture and Terror Held America Captive 22 Years Ago." *Entertainment Weekly* (September 12, 1997), p. 152.

Here's a book you might like:

Every Secret Thing, 1982, by Patty Hearst and Alvin Moscow

Hearst gives a first-person account of her ordeal in this autobiography. "It's a personal story," she says, "and I hope it will give people the feeling of what happened and how they might react in the same situation. I want people to understand what I experienced."

Hearst has also published a novel (which was co-written with Cornelia Frances Biddle). *Murder at San Simeon,* published in 1996, is a mystery based on some 1924 events at the mansion of multi-millionaire William Randolph Hearst Jr., the newspaper heiress's grandfather.

Marion Hedgepeth

Born: ?
Died: January 1, 1910

Operating at the end of the era of American train robbers, Marion Hedgepeth enjoyed a certain degree of popularity until he was shot and killed in a botched robbery attempt.

THE HEDGEPETH FOUR

Born and raised in Cooper County, Missouri, Hedgepeth headed West as a teenager in hopes of becoming a cowboy. He traveled to Colorado, Montana, and Wyoming, and by the 1880s had earned a reputation as a robber, rustler, and killer. An expert shooter, he reportedly had lightning-fast reflexes. It was said that he could draw and shoot a man who had *already* drawn a pistol on him.

By 1890, Hedgepeth had formed a group of outlaws known to lawmen as the "Hedgepeth Four." The gang included Hedgepeth, Charles "Dink" Burke, James "Illinois Jimmy" Francis, and Albert "Bertie" Sly. After committing a number of holdups and muggings, the gang pulled their first train robbery on November 4, 1890. Stopping the Missouri Pacific train near Omaha, Nebraska, they got away with about $1,000. The following week they headed to Wisconsin, where they robbed the Chicago, Milwaukee & St. Paul train line just outside of Milwaukee on November 12, 1890. Without pausing to allow the guard to surrender, they dynamited the express car in order to get at its contents. The gang ran away from the wrecked railway car with $5,000. The express guard somehow survived the ordeal.

Within weeks, the gang organized another robbery. After boarding a St. Louis train, they stopped it near Glendale, Missouri. Without firing a shot, they emptied the express car safe of $50,000—their most successful haul ever. Leaving the site, the gang members deliberately created trails that would mislead the detectives who followed them. They returned to St. Louis and rented rooms to wait for the posse (a group of people with legal authority to capture criminals) activity to die down.

But the Hedgepeth Four had made a fatal mistake. Before retreating to St. Louis, they had buried their weapons—and envelopes that had contained the money from their last theft—inside a shed. Shortly after the robbery, a young girl who was playing in the shed dug up the evidence. The newly discovered clues enabled lawmen to trace Hedgepeth to his room in St. Louis.

JAILED IN ST. LOUIS

Awaiting trial in St. Louis, Hedgepeth was a bit of a celebrity. A slim, six-foot-tall man, he was a sharp dresser who wore well-tailored suits, a derby hat over slicked-back hair, and a large wing collar with a cravat, or tie, that was kept in place by a diamond stick-pin. Women admirers reportedly sent him flowers as he waited for the trial to begin.

Held in a St. Louis jail until his trial, Hedgepeth shared a cell for a while with a man who called himself Harry Howard Holmes. Imprisoned on a swindling charge (obtaining money through cheating a person), Holmes asked Hedgepeth to recommend a good attorney—for a fee. In exchange for a promise to pay $500, Hedgepeth introduced Holmes to a well-respected criminal attorney named J. D. Howe. Soon released from jail on bail, Holmes did not pay Hedgepeth the money he had promised. But he did confide details of his criminal activity to Hedgepeth—a big mistake that would later haunt him.

NO SURRENDER

After a long delay and much publicity, Hedgepeth's trial was held in 1892. He was convicted and sentenced to twelve to

The legend of Herman Webster Mudgett

Harry Howard Holmes was one of the many aliases (fake names) used by Herman W. Mudgett. Born and raised in Gilmantown, New Hampshire, he attended medical school at the University of Michigan. There he discovered an easy way to make money. After taking out large insurance policies under various names, he stole corpses (dead bodies) from the medical school's dissecting rooms. Having taken care to burn the bodies—and then using acid to dispose of the parts that would not burn— to keep them from being correctly identified, he then left the cadavers where they would eventually be discovered. Once his victim was officially pronounced dead, he collected the insurance money. Mudgett collected a small fortune before he was caught pilfering (stealing) the body of a young woman, for which he was expelled (kicked-out) from school.

Mudgett drifted to Chicago, where he took a job in a drugstore. Having saved enough money, he hired builders to construct a three-story structure that had trap doors, concealed rooms, hidden stairways, and doorways that led to brick walls. The basement was equipped with a large dissecting table, an immense stove, and a couple of pits.

twenty-five years in the state penitentiary (prison). After he had served only a few years of the sentence, some important Missourians began to work to have him released. Double-crossed by his former cell-mate, Hedgepeth had informed on Holmes. Because he had been an important witness in Holmes's conviction, Hedgepeth was praised as a "friend of society." In spite of the these efforts, the campaign to release Hedgepeth was unsuccessful. The train robber remained in prison until July 1906, by which time he had become very ill with tuberculosis (a deadly disease that affects the lungs).

One year and two months after his release, Hedgepeth was arrested for robbing a safe in Omaha, Nebraska. Caught in the act, he was sentenced to two more years in prison. After he was released, he organized another gang of robbers. They pulled a number of small robberies in the West, and Hedgepeth eventually drifted to Chicago, Illinois. On January 1, 1910, he pulled a gun on a saloon owner and robbed the cash register. A policeman saw the robbery and drew his gun, demanding that Hedgepeth surrender. The robber reportedly coughed once and shouted, "Never!" Hedgepeth and the policeman shot at the same time, but only the robber was hit. Struck in the chest by a

Claiming to be a businessman in need of secretarial help, Mudgett contacted several employment agencies. Once a young woman was sent to work for him, he reportedly convinced her that he wanted to marry her—and that she should sign over her belongings to him. Once the young woman complied (agreed), he killed her—and dissected the body in the basement. The stove was sometimes used to burn the bodies, while the pits, filled with quicklime, burned them beyond recognition. Many murders later, Mudgett became discouraged because his earnings were not what he had hoped. He set the building on fire, expecting to collect an insurance settlement.

When police officials insisted on examining the building's remains, Mudgett left town. He eventually arrived in St. Louis, where a simple swindle landed him in jail. Calling himself Harry Howard Holmes, he shared a jail cell with Marion Hedgepeth, who was awaiting the start of his trial.

Mudgett eventually confessed in detail to the murders he had committed at his Chicago residence, which became known as Murder Castle. He described the killings in his "memoirs" (a book about a person's life), which went unfinished. On May 7, 1896, he was hanged.

bullet, he fell to his knees, fired his gun's remaining bullets into the ground, and died.

Sources for Further Reading

McLoughlin, Denis. *Wild and Woolly, An Encyclopedia of the Old West.* New York: Doubleday, 1975, pp. 218–219.

Nash, Jay Robert. *Bloodletters and Badmen.* New York: M. Evans, 1973, pp. 252, 382–387.

Nash, Jay Robert. *The Encyclopedia of World Crime.* Wilmette, IL: Crime Books, 1990, p. 1506.

Bill Miner

Born: 1846
Died: September 2, 1913
AKA: George Budd, California Bill,
George Edwards, John Luck, William Morgan

In a career that spanned from the Civil War years (1861–1865) to the twentieth century, Bill Miner robbed trains and stagecoaches in five states and Canada. Regarded as a gentleman robber, he spent much of his life behind bars.

A FICTIONAL LIFE

Imprisoned toward the end of his life, Miner recorded his life story while serving a sentence in a Georgia jail. His autobiography (the story his life) provided contemporary newspapers with engaging stories of his bandit exploits and later writers with ample material for detailed biographies. The trouble was, Miner was a bit of a storyteller.

Miner claimed to have been born in Kentucky in 1847. Deserted by his father at the age of ten, he ran away from home when he was thirteen to become a cowboy. After a daring trip across land that was populated by hostile Apache Indians, he started up a daring one-man pony express business. Unable to support himself with his earnings, he became a criminal—finding time in between jobs to travel the world.

But Miner's story doesn't match historical records. One of several children, he was born near Onondaga, in Ingham County, Michigan in 1846. After his father died, Miner—who was still a boy—moved with his mother, Harriet J. Miner, to Yankee

Jims, a gold-mining town in Placer County, California. There he earned miserable pay working as a laborer. In his teens, Miner enlisted in the Union Army as a private with the California Cavalry Volunteers. His military career was short-lived: on July 22, 1864, less than three months after he had enlisted, he deserted his post.

"ON THE ROB"

By December of 1865, Miner was, as he told one of his victims, "on the rob." After renting a horse several miles outside of Yankee Jims, he rode to the town of Auburn, where he stole an expensive suit and a store clerk's watch. He rode back to the mining camp and never returned the rented horse. Heading for San Francisco, he met a fifteen- year-old named John Sinclair. Together they "rented" two more horses and, on January 22, 1866, held up a ranch-hand named Porter as he drove a wagon near Stockton. Although Porter told the robbers he had no money, he eventually handed over $80— $10 of which Miner returned so that Porter could buy new boots.

By evening, Porter had informed the police of the holdup. Captured the following morning—as they slept in a hotel— Miner and Sinclair were taken into custody at the Stockton County jail. They attempted to escape by digging their way out of jail, but a wall reinforced by a metal plate defeated their effort. Tried after one month in jail, they were convicted of armed robbery. Miner and Sinclair were each sentenced to three years' imprisonment. On April 5, 1866, Miner entered San Quentin penitentiary. In the meantime, however, he had been tried for horse theft. Convicted of grand larceny, he landed another five-year sentence at the San Quentin prison.

Guilty verdict overturned

Captured shortly after they robbed a stagecoach near San Andreas, California, Miner and Harrington were taken to a jail in Calveras County to await trial. There, they were chained to the floor of the cell with forty-pound irons. Harrington managed to saw through his irons—and had started to work on Miner's fetters (another name for iron chains)—before the guards found out.

To prevent their escape, Miner and Harrington were forced to wear heavy iron chains in court when they were tried. Later, their ten-year sentences were appealed and overturned. The California Supreme Court ruled that they hadn't received a fair trial: because they wore chains, the jury was more inclined to find them guilty. On March 21, Miner and Harrington were tried again—and convicted. Each was committed to thirteen years in prison—adding four years to their original sentences.

Read all about it!

After having been convicted of armed robbery and horse theft, Miner and his accomplice were sentenced to three years in the San Quentin penitentiary. Boarding a steamship that was to take them to prison, they acted as if they were about to embark on a pleasure cruise. Here's how a local newspaper described their departure:

John Sinclair and William Miner were taken off, in charge of Deputy Sheriff J. M. Long, on the steamer *Julia* yesterday, en route for San Quentin to serve a term of three years for highway robbery. The prisoners were chained together, and stood on the upper dock until the steamer left the wharf. They were jovial and appeared unconcerned. When the steamer moved off they threw apples into the crowd on the wharf, and waved their pocket handkerchiefs, as if bidding adieu [goodbye] to friends.

—**The Stockton Daily Independent**

While serving his term at the penitentiary, Miner became friends with another prisoner—"Alkali Jim" Harrington, a burglar and stagecoach robber who was serving his third term at San Quentin. After serving a little over four years of his sentence, Miner was released from San Quentin on July 12, 1870. Together with Harrington, who had been released before him, he participated in a number of burglaries and robberies in northern and southern California.

In January of 1871, Miner returned to stagecoach robbery. First Miner, Harrington, and a young Easterner named Charlie Cooper broke into a hardware store to steal shotguns and pistols. Then they traveled to San Andreas, where Miner studied the comings and goings of local stagecoaches. On January 23 they struck. After Miner stopped the coach, pretending to need a ride, Cooper and Harrington stepped in front of the horse team—with shotguns aimed at the driver. Miner then directed the driver to throw down the Wells Fargo strongbox. Taking a hatchet (small axe) to the box, the robbers collected more than $2,500 in gold dust and coins.

But Miner hadn't worn a mask. By June—after less than one year of freedom—he was back behind the walls of San Quentin. Tried on June 22, Miner and Harrington were each sentenced to ten years in the state prison. Cooper—who had informed on his companions by turning state's evidence—was not convicted.

OLD HABITS DIE HARD

After serving nine years, Miner was released on July 14,

1880. Shortly after he headed to Colorado Springs—to see his older sister, Mary Jane Wellman—he met an Iowa farm worker named Arthur Pond. The pair staged a number of coach robberies. In less than one month, they pulled three holdups which yielded thousands of dollars in loot.

Traveling to Michigan with his share of the booty—and suitcases full of new clothes—Miner posed as a successful California businessman named William A. Morgan. He stayed in Onondaga at the Sherman House, the town's finest hotel, and became engaged to marry a young woman from a prosperous family. In February 1881, he left abruptly, claiming that his ill mother needed him.

Miner returned to Colorado, where he rejoined Pond—who now went by the alias (fake name) of Billy LeRoy—and Pond's brother, Silas. After the threesome pulled two more stagecoach robberies, they were hunted by a posse (a group of people with legal authority to capture criminals). The Pond brothers were captured. In jail awaiting trial, they were lynched (killed illegally) by angry locals who broke into their cell. Miner—who had gone into town to retrieve supplies—remained at large.

Joining forces with Stanton T. Jones, Miner continued to rob stages in Colorado and New Mexico. In California the two hooked up with Jim Crum—Miner's friend from San Quentin—and Bill Miller, who was part of Crum's successful gang of horse thieves. Early in the morning of November 7, the newly formed gang stopped a stagecoach near Angels Camp. Armed and masked, the robbers referred to each other by numbers to avoid being identified. Breaking open two Wells Fargo strongboxes and a safe, they found more than $3,000 in gold—to which they added another $500 worth of gold dust that a passenger had hidden.

No Exit

Pursued by lawmen from five counties, Miner and two others were soon captured. On December 21, 1881, Miner returned to San Quentin—after having spent less than a year and a half

> ## Take a look at this!
>
> Loosely based on the story of Bill Miner, *The Grey Fox* (1983) follows a gentlemanly old stagecoach robber as he tries to pick up his life after thirty years in prison—as he is suddenly thrown into the twentieth century. Unable to resist another heist, he tries train robbery, and winds up hiding out in British Columbia.

"Hands up!"
According to the Pinkerton detectives who pursued him, Miner was the first bandit to use the phrase "Hands up!" in a robbery.

Hard time

San Quentin, referred to as "the Stones," was a brutal prison in Miner's day. Prisoners faced a number of inhumane punishments—including whippings and "showers" that consisted of being blasted in the face by a high-pressure water hose. Convicts were often thrown into the dungeon—a dank, dark, filthy hole with no windows or fresh air. Fed meager rations of bread and water, they slept on the dungeon's cold stone floor.

Prison reforms that brought about slightly more humane conditions gradually crept into the Stones. In 1864—two years before Miner's first trip to prison—the Goodwin Act allowed prisoners time off their sentences for good behavior. Prisoners accumulated "coppers," or credits, that were subtracted from the prison sentence. After 1880, prisoners were no longer whipped, and the practice of "showering" ended two years later. The dungeon, however, was not abandoned until after Miner had served three separate terms at San Quentin.

in freedom. Before he had served the first year of his sentence, Miner attempted to escape—*twice.* In his second attempt, on November 29, 1892, Miner and his cellmate, Joe Marshall, managed to escape onto a balcony that surrounded their cell block. Ambushed by guards who knew of their plans, they were fired on with no warning. Marshall was shot dead and Miner was wounded.

Miner later described the shooting in an interview:

[Marshall] opened the door and looked out and nobody was to be seen. Then we slid out and started toward the steps. There was no guard in sight and we calculated to slip by one man in a guardhouse near where we had to go down the steps. Joe was ahead and I was close behind. Just as we got to the corner of the stone building and Joe had gone down a step or two the shot came and you bet it was a surprise when I hear that gun. Joe tumbled down and I started to run, but the guard sent in another shot and I did not know much for some time after. . . . The guard did not call out or make any noise to let us know he was there. If he had we should have gotten back to 47 [the number of their cell], because it is no use to go up against buckshot.

In spite of his efforts to flee, Miner received time off his sentence for good behavior. (On one occasion, he helped put out a fire in the shop building.) On June 17, 1901—eight years, five months, and nineteen days after his last failed attempt to escape—Miner left San Quentin a free man. He never returned.

Oh, Canada!

A grey-haired man of fifty-five, Miner could no longer support himself as a stagecoach robber—not because of his age, but because stagecoaches had become outdated. During his long stay at San Quentin, he took advantage of the resources at hand to learn a new trade: jailed with a number of experienced train robbers, Miner learned what he could about their methods.

A little more than two years after his release from prison, Miner and two others held up the Oregon Railway and Navigation Company express train. He then moved north to Canada, with Jake Terry, a counterfeiter who had shared a cell with him at San Quentin. A former railway engineer, Terry was familiar with Canadian train routes. Miner and Terry plotted to rob a train near Mission Junction in British Columbia. First, they tapped the telegraph lines to find out which trains carried large shipments of gold. On September 13, 1904, Miner, Terry, and a man named Shorty Dunn struck the Canadian Pacific railway's transcontinental express forty miles outside of Vancouver. The gang collected thousands of dollars in gold dust and currency. They also pocketed $50,000 in U.S. bonds that were being shipped to Seattle—in addition to thousands of dollars in Australian securities.

His next Canadian train robbery was far less successful than the first. On May 8, 1906, Miner held up the Canadian Pacific's Imperial Limited near Kamloops, British Columbia. He left with about $15—and a handful of cough tablets. Six days later, Miner and two of his accomplices were captured by the Royal North-West Mounted Police.

Tried and convicted, Miner was sentenced to life imprisonment at the New Westminster penitentiary in British Columbia.

A staged escape?

Sometime after Miner escaped from the New Westminster prison in British Columbia, local newspapers claimed that the train robber had been *allowed* to escape. A number of things made Miner's disappearance look suspicious. First, Miner had met with detectives during the weeks prior to his escape. After the escape, police officials claimed that no man could have crawled through the tunnel the convict had supposedly used. What's more, Miner had a foot injury that would have limited his mobility.

Journalists suggested that Miner had worked out a deal with Canadian officials: freedom in exchange for the bonds he had stolen from the Canadian Pacific railway in September 1904. Although the matter was debated in the Canadian Parliament, Miner's escape was never fully investigated by the Canadian government. And Miner never confessed.

First and last

Miner's career began in the Civil War era—and ended in the twentieth century with an automobile ride to jail. Even in his day, he was considered to be one of the last frontier outlaws. But he was also known for a number of firsts: he is credited with having committed the first train robbery in the state of Georgia. And he was the *first* robber ever to hold up a train in all of Canada.

Popular with many local people who despised the railroads, he became a bit of a celebrity: large crowds surrounded him after the trial. Some admirers even tossed him cigars. Miner served less than one year of his sentence at the New Westminster prison. On August 8, 1907, he escaped.

TIME TO RETIRE

At the age of sixty-four, Miner committed his last train robbery—the first ever in the state of Georgia. Working with two accomplices, he struck a Southern Express train at White Sulfur Springs on February 22, 1911. A couple of thousand dollars richer, the three men were hunted by local and federal lawmen. Within a few days, Miner faced a twenty-year sentence at a state prison.

On March 15, Miner was sent to work on a chain gang at Newton County Convict Camp. Claiming that he was old and in ill health, he petitioned the prison commission to transfer him to a low-security prison farm in Milledgeville. With the help of public support, he was transferred. Within months, he escaped.

Just over two weeks later, Miner was captured and returned to Milledgeville, where he was met by crowds of locals. Eight months later, on June 29, 1912, he escaped again. After three days in the Georgia swamps, Miner was captured. Again he was greeted by cheering crowds. Back in prison, Miner reportedly told guards, "I guess I'm getting too old for this sort of thing." On September 2, 1913, he died in the prison hospital.

Sources for Further Reading

Boessenecker, John. *Badge and Buckshot, Lawlessness in Old California.* Norman, OK: University of Oklahoma Press, 1988, pp. 158–177.

Bruns, Roger. *The Bandit Kings from Jesse James to Pretty Boy Floyd.* New York: Crown, 1995, pp. 132–133.

Dugan, Mark and John Boessenecker. *Grey Fox: The True Story of Bill Miner, Last of the Old-Time Bandits.* Norman, OK: University of Oklahoma Press, 1992.

Irene Schroeder

Born: 1909
Died: February 23, 1931

*Irene Schroeder's career shared many things with that of two more famous outlaws. But she enjoyed none of the notoriety that surrounded **Bonnie and Clyde** (see entry). A minor robber, Schroeder became most famous after death—as one of very few women to have been put to death in the electric chair.*

ONE DEAD COP

Toward the end of 1929, when she was a twenty–year–old housewife, Schroeder met a salesman and Sunday school teacher named Walter Glenn Dague. She left her husband to accompany Dague, who deserted his wife and children in West Virginia. Traveling in a stolen car with Schroeder's four–year–old son, Donnie, the couple robbed a number of stores and small banks.

Schroeder and Dague's final robbery took place in Butler, Pennsylvania. After robbing a grocery store, they left by car—and were soon chased by two highway patrolmen, Ernest Moore and W. Brady Paul. With Donnie in the back seat of the car, Dague and Schroeder fired at the patrolmen as they sped through the Pennsylvania countryside. Patrolman Paul was killed by a bullet Schroeder had fired and Moore was wounded by Dague. The patrolmen's car veered off the road and into a ditch.

The outlaw couple managed to avoid capture—in spite of road blocks that had been erected by police. Hundreds of miles south, in Arizona, they were finally surrounded by a posse (a

The death penalty

Not all countries that embrace capital punishment (the death penalty) permit the execution of women. Russia, for example, excludes women from the death penalty.

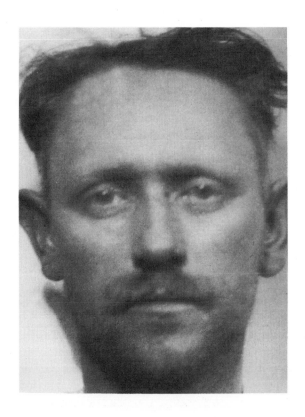

Walter Dague,
Schroeder's
partner-in-crime.

group of people with legal authority to capture criminals) as they traveled down a back road. A shootout followed. Eventually—after they had run out of bullets—Schroeder and Dague surrendered.

TRIED, CONVICTED, AND EXECUTED

Tried for the murder of patrolman Paul, Schroeder admitted that she was guilty—and she tried to claim that she had been responsible for the robberies and other crimes that Dague had committed with her. Her attempt to save Dague failed. Both were convicted and sentenced to be executed.

Schroeder was taken to the Rockview Penitentiary in Center County, Pennsylvania, to await execution. On February 23, 1931, a prison chaplain visited her before she was led to the electric chair. She reportedly told him, that she would be all right—but that he should check on Dague, who needed the clergyman more than she did. Just before she died she is said to have had a final request: that prison cooks prepare Dague's eggs the way he liked them—fried on both sides. Schroeder died in the electric chair less than three minutes after the current was administered. She was the first of only two women to have been electrocuted in the state of Pennsylvania. Dague was executed a few days later.

From the mouths of babes

Donnie Schroeder, the bandit-murderer's young son, reportedly told a policeman "My mother killed a cop like you." The four-year-old was a state's witness at his mother's trial.

Sources for Further Reading

Kadish, Sanford, ed. *Encyclopedia of Crime and Justice,* Volume 1. New York: Free Press, 1983, pp.133–142.

Nash, Jay Robert. *Look for the Woman: A Narrative Encyclopedia of Female Poisoners, Kidnappers, Thieves, Extortionists, Terrorists, Swindlers, and Spies from Elizabethan Times to Present.* New York: Evans, 1981, pp. 339–341.

Sifakis, Carl. *The Encyclopedia of American Crime.* New York: Facts on File, 1982, pp.238–240.

A public spectacle

In 1824, a hatchet murderer named John Johnson was hanged in New York City. The event was a public spectacle. Later, newspapers reported that fifty thousand people had attended Johnson's hanging. At the time, executions—and hangings, in particular—had a long history as public entertainment. Pirate hangings, which were intended to serve as a warning to others, often attracted enormous crowds. In the Old West, hangings were sometimes scheduled on weekends to guarantee a well-attended execution. Far from a solemn event, hangings were the cause for celebration.

Today, executions are always performed behind prison walls. But public executions were not outlawed until the 1930s. The final public executions in the United States took place in 1936, when a man was hanged in Kentucky for rape, and 1937, when a murderer was hanged in Missouri.

Since television was introduced in the 1950s, some people have argued in favor of televised executions. They believe that televised executions—like public hangings—would serve as a deterrent (a preventive measure) to other would-be criminals. Others—who oppose capital punishment—support televised executions as a means to turn the public against what they believe to be an inhumane practice. In 1977, the federal courts considered whether prison authorities in Texas should be forced to allow public television to cover an execution. The courts decided against television coverage.

Still, there is a public aspect to many executions. When Karla Faye Tucker was executed in February 1998, hundreds gathered outside the Huntsville, Texas, institution where she died. Some were protesting the taking of a life. Others, in the spirit of the bygone revelers who attended pirate hangings and outlaw executions, were there to see the show—and to express their approval of the ax murderer's fate. One person carried a sign that said, "Axe and ye shall receive." When officials announced that Tucker was dead, the crowd let out a cheer. Some cried, while others sang the song whose refrain is "Na na na na, hey, hey, hey, goodbye."

Veitz, Dee Tabone. *Irene.* Punxsatawney, PA: Spirit, 1985.

Verhovek, Sam Howe. "Dead Women Waiting: Who's on Death Row." *The New York Times* (February 8, 1998), pp. A1, 3, 17.

Index

Italic type indicates volume number;
boldface *indicates main entries and their page numbers;*
(ill.) indicates illustration.

L

La Guardia, Fiorello *3:* 456
LaCroix, Peter *3:* 473
"The Lady in Red." *See* Sage, Anna
Lake Valley Gang *3:* 419
Lamm, Herman K. *1:* 131, 138
Lamphere, Ray *1:* 146–147, 149
Lancaster, Roscoe *1:* 130
Lansky, Meyer *1:* 24, **47–52**, 47 (ill.), 57–58, 71, 82, 91; *3:* 442
Last Exit to Brooklyn *1:* 94
Lawes, Nicholas *3:* 490
Lawrence Berkeley Laboratory *2:* 184
Lay, Elza *3:* 371
Leavenworth Prison *1:* 76
Lebowitz, Joe *1:* 55
Lee, Andrew Daulton *2:* 224–229, 226 (ill.)
Legalized gambling *1:* 62
Leigh, Jennifer Jason *1:* 94
Leonatti, Philip *1:* 87
Lepke, Louis *1:* 60, 78–79, **89–95**, 89 (ill.)
LeRoy, Billy. *See* Pond, Arthur
"Letter of Marque" *3:* 481. *See also* Treaty of Utrecht (1713)
Lewis, Frank "Jumbo" *1:* 130
Lewis, George *1:* 55
Lewis-Jones Gang *1:* 131–132
Liberty Park Tots Gang *1:* 35
Life magazine *2:* 275
Lincoln, Abraham *2:* 242
Lincoln County War *3:* 348
Little, Russell *1:* 158
Little Bohemia Lodge shootout *1:* 141
"Little Jerusalem" *1:* 53
"Little Jewish Navy" *1:* 55
"Little Louis." *See* Lepke, Louis
Logan, Harvey *3:* 368 (ill.), 371
Lombroso, Caesar *2:* 288
Long, Huey E. *1:* 70
Longabaugh, Harry. *See* The Sundance Kid

Los Alamos National Labortory *2:* 200
The Losers *2:* 271
Luciano, Lucky *1:* 13, 23, 48–49, 57, 82, 91–92
Luck, John. *See* Miner, Bill
Lyons, Ned *2:* 281
Lyons, Sophie *2:* **281–286**

M

Machine Gun Kelly *3:* 436
Madden, Owney *1:* 68; *3:* **437–442**, 437 (ill.), 441, 454
Madero, Francisco *3:* 411
Mail fraud *1:* 12; *2:* 295
Makley, Charles *1:* 137
"The Man Uptown." *See* Rothstein, Arnold
Mangano, Vincent *1:* 23
Manhattan Project *2:* 237
Manning, Frank *3:* 404, 408
Manning, George "Doc" *3:* 404, 408
Manning, Jim *3:* 404, 408
Maranzano, Salvatore *1:* 21
Marchese, Carmela *1:* 86
Marcus, Josephine Sarah *3:* 385
Married to the Mob *1:* 46
Marshall, James Wilson *3:* 338
Marshall, Joe *1:* 174
Martin, Steve *2:* 301
Martynov, Valeri *2:* 218–219
Masotto, Thomas *1:* 21
Massacres *1:* 17, 19, 55–56; *3:* 413–414, 423, 447
Masseria, Joseph *1:* 21
Masterson, Bartholomew "Bat" *3:* 334–336, 336 (ill.)
Matthews, Gene *2:* 313
Matthews, Martha *2:* 185
Maverick Law *2:* 255
Maxwell, Kate. *See* Cattle Kate
May, John *1:* 19
Maynard, Robert *3:* 481, 483 (ill.)
McBratney, James *1:* 36
McCarty, Henry. *See* Billy the Kid

McCarty Gang *3:* 369
McClellan Committee *1:* 4
McConnell, Ann *2:* 289
McCormick, Jane Hickok *3:* 362
McCulloch, Frank *2:* 275
McDonald, Joe *1:* 80
McGraw, John *1:* 96
McGraw-Hill Publishing Company *2:* 272
MCI *2:* 198
McManus, George *1:* 99, 101
McMullin, Freddie *1:* 97
McVeigh, Timothy *2:* **315–324**, 315 (ill.), 317 (ill.)
"McVeigh Bill" *2:* 321
Meeks, Bob *3:* 371
Mercedes River *3:* 338
Merchants National Bank scam *2:* 299
Methvin, Henry *1:* 126
Mexican Revolution *3:* 410
Meyer Lansky, Mogul of the Mob *1:* 48
Milaflores Massacre *1:* 55
Milberg, Irving *1:* 56
Milnet (computer network) *2:* 185. *See also* Computer hacking
Mimms, Zerelda *3:* 389
Miner, Bill *1:* **170–176**
Mink, George *2:* 233–234
Mitnick, Kevin *2:* **197–204**, 197 (ill.)
Mobster books
    Billy Bathgate *1:* 74
    Family Blood *1:* 34
    Most Precious Blood *1:* 26
Mobster funerals *3:* 468
Mobster movies
    Bonnie & Clyde *1:* 123
    Bugsy *1:* 46, 62
    Bugsy Malone *3:* 469
    Dillinger *1:* 143
    The Godfather *1:* 25
    The Godfather, Part II *1:* 52
    Hoodlum *1:* 33
    Last Exit to Brooklyn *1:* 94
    Machine Gun Kelly *3:* 436